THE TEA COOKBOOK

OTHER COOKBOOKS BY
WILLIAM I. KAUFMAN

THE ART OF CREOLE COOKERY

THE ART OF INDIA'S COOKERY

THE COFFEE COOKBOOK

THE NUT COOKBOOK

THE I LOVE PEANUT BUTTER COOKBOOK

THE HOT DOG COOKBOOK

THE CATHOLIC COOKBOOK

COOKING IN A CASTLE

THE WONDERFUL WORLD OF COOKING SERIES
Near East-Far East
Italy, France & Spain
Northern European and the British Isles
Caribbean and Latin America

THE STAND UP COOKBOOK SERIES
Quick and Easy Desserts
Budget Cooking for Company
Casserole Cooking
The Left Over Cookbook

THE SUGAR FREE COOKBOOK

THE SUGAR FREE COOKBOOK OF FAMILY FAVORITES

THE

TEA

COOKBOOK

WILLIAM I. KAUFMAN

DOUBLEDAY & COMPANY, INC.

GARDEN CITY, NEW YORK, 1966

The author wishes to thank
The Lipton Kitchens and *The Tea Council of the U.S.A.*
for their cooperation.

Photos courtesy of The Lipton Kitchens

Library of Congress Catalog Card Number 66–20952
Copyright © 1966 by William I. Kaufman
All Rights Reserved
Printed in the United States of America
First Edition

THE TEA COOKBOOK

is dedicated to my wife

who makes life a joy

CONTENTS

THE ROMANTIC LEGENDS AND
EARLY HISTORY OF TEA

The origin of tea, called "The Gift of Heaven" by the Chinese, is wrapped tightly in the silken cocoon of legend. Discovered in China untold centuries ago, the tree was identified with the names of other shrubs. It was thus variously known from the year 2737 B.C., when the legendary Emperor Shen Nung, called the Divine Healer, mentioned it in his medical observations entitled *Pen ts'ao* along with several other medicinal plants. In 350 A.D. the first reliable reference to tea was made in the *Erh Ya*, an early Chinese dictionary written by the celebrated scholar Kuo P'o. The *Erh Ya* defines *kia* or *k'u t'u* as "a beverage made from the leaves by boiling"—the first recognizable definition of tea.

Today this beverage is imbibed more than any other liquid save water and is considered the favorite drink of athletes and scholars, outdoorsmen and poets.

Three fascinating legends of tea have survived all the centuries, even though scholars admit that we shall probably never know when tea was actually first used as a beverage or how and when the cultivation of this plant had its beginning.

Legend of Shen Nung, 2737 B.C.

The fable of Shen Nung recounts for us the story of how the great Emperor observed that people who boiled their drink-

9

ing water enjoyed better health. Shen Nung followed this regimen even while traveling. The legend goes on to say that the wise man asked his servants to make a fire so that his drinking water might be purified while he was en route to a foreign province. As the Divine Healer knelt before the fire, waiting for the water to boil, a light breeze blew some of the uppermost leaves from the branches of firewood into the pot. The Emperor, attracted by the fragrance of the liquid, tasted the brew and pronounced it delicious.

In his observations on medical subjects, not actually written down until the Neo-Han dynasty (25–221 A.D.), Shen Nung proclaimed the beverage's attributes: "good for tumors or abscesses that come about the head, or for ailments of the bladder. It dissipates heat caused by the phlegms, or inflammation of the chest . . . quenches thirst . . . lessens the desire for sleep . . . gladdens and cheers the heart. . . ."

Interestingly enough, these age-old claims for the efficacy of tea still seem to hold true to some degree.

With the Legend of Shen Nung the Chinese acclaim the discovery of their precious steaming liquid.

The drink was at first used only as a medicinal decoction. The *Kuang Ya*, a dictionary written by Chang I in the Later Wei dynasty (386–535 A.D.), tells us how the medicine was prepared. It was the practice to pluck the tea leaves and make them into reddish-colored cakes. In the making of tea, these cakes were pounded into small pieces and placed in a chinaware pot. Boiling water was poured over the tea morsels and onion, ginger, and orange were added to hide the bitterness.

By the fifth century a great transition took place in the use of tea. Although it continued in high repute as a remedy, its use as a drink gained in esteem. By 780 A.D. the great *Ch'a Ching*, or "Tea Book," was written by Lu Yu, noted Chinese tea expert whose adventurous life included a childhood among Buddhist priests, a youthful career as a famous clown, and a maturity spent in scholarship dedicated to the study of tea cultivation, tea manufacture, and tea drinking. Under the patronage of the great Chinese tea merchants Lu Yu wrote the *Ch'a Ching* in three volumes, with ten parts, which dealt with the nature of the tea plant and the utensils necessary for the gathering and preserving of tea. It described, with illustrations, the twenty-four implements needed for the tea ceremony—an eloquent ritual which was the result of Lu Yu's meditation and mature philosophical thoughts on the subject of tea. The *Ch'a Ching* also contained detailed information on the methods of tea making and tea drinking, a historical summary of tea legends, an enumeration of important tea-growing plantations, and information about tea preservation. Centuries later, enterprising Dutch and English businessmen were able to establish their great tea empires with the information given by this ancient scholarly classic.

After the writing of the *Ch'a Ching*, tea came into general use and soon thereafter was recognized as a substantial source of revenue by the Emperors of the T'ang dynasty (618–907 A. D.), who were the first to levy duties on tea.

Whipped tea made its primary appearance in the Sung dynasty (960–1279 A.D.). The fashion in which the tea was made is remarkably similar to the principles we use today when we make instant tea. Tea leaves were dried and ground into a fine powder. The powder was mixed with fresh boiling water and whipped with a light bamboo whisk. During this era the custom of using additives with tea definitely disappeared and the beverage was enjoyed for its special purity and delicacy of flavor and aroma.

Tea epicures became numerous. New varieties of tea were eagerly sought. Tournaments were frequently held in which the merits of the different varieties of tea were judged. Elaborate teahouses were established in all the cities of China. The cultivation of tea spread throughout the provinces and came to the attention of travelers from abroad. China became the fountainhead for the tea culture which spread throughout the entire world.

The Legend of Gan Lu

The second great tea legend tells us that in the Han dynasty (208 B.C.–220 A.D.) Gan Lu, a great Buddhist scholar, returned from his studies in India bringing with him seven tea plants which he radicated on the Meng Mountain in Szechwan, and from which all future tea plants were said to have sprung.

Though this legend has been discredited, this mention of India as the "home" of tea spotlights a mystery which confounded students of the subject for many centuries—whether tea originated in China or in India.

Extensive research now shows us that the tea plant is in point of fact indigenous to both countries. Nature itself established a "tea garden" in the monsoon district of Southeastern Asia. Specimens of the original wild tea plant can still be found in Northern Thailand, Eastern Burma, the Unnan and Szechwan districts of China, upper parts of Laos and Viet Nam, as well as in India. It is thus evident that before these lands were divided into separate states by man, a primeval tea garden existed in which the conditions of soil, climate, and rainfall were perfectly balanced for the propagation of the wild tea—an evergreen plant which grows best in a continuously hot, wet climate with high humidity. It has been established that the first recorded cultivation of tea took place in China around the year 350 A.D. and spread down the Yangtze Valley and throughout the provinces. The cultivation of tea in India, however, was unknown until 1832. Before that year Great Britain, unaware of the indigenous tea plants, tried to import Chinese tea plants into India and set up a tea industry. Incapable of thinking of anything but China tea, the English traveled thousands of miles to China for seeds, plants, and workmen to try experiments which failed again and again. But in 1823 Major Robert Bruce conducted a trading expedition and reported the discovery of native tea trees in Assam. His findings were confirmed a year later by his brother, C. A. Bruce, the real founder of tea cultivation in Assam and the first to urge recognition of the native "jat" or tea seedling. In 1831 Captain Andrew Charlton reported wild tea trees growing near Beesa, in Assam. Yet it was only after the East India Company's monopoly of the China tea trade was broken in 1833 that India tea received the attention it merited.

In 1834 a committee was formed by Governor General Lord William Charles Cavendish Bentinck which signaled the founding of the far-flung kingdom of India tea—a kingdom which extends to all countries of the world where tea is grown or used as a beverage. Tea cultivation spread rapidly after Mr. Bruce showed its commercial potential. Today, the Assam jat, so long ignored, is responsible for the powerful and profitable tea industries of Ceylon and Indonesia.

The Bodhidharma Legend

The third of the tea legends is to be found in Japanese mythology. It attributes the origin of tea in China to the great "White Buddha," Daruma, or Bodhidharma as he is known in India. According to the fable, Daruma slumbered during one of his meditations. Upon awakening, the beloved saint was so ashamed at his transgression that he cut off his eyelids. The legend records that as the fallen eyelids lay on the ground they took root and grew up as tea plants.

Tea is so much a part of the culture of Japan that the country's historians cannot conceive of a time in which this lovely, slender, green-leafed tree, pruned to a height of five feet and covered with fragrant white blossoms resembling wild roses, did not flourish in their temple gardens.

The annals record that the Japanese Emperor Shomu bestowed a gift of powdered tea upon a hundred Buddhist priests who came to the Imperial Palace to read the scriptures to him in 729 A.D. Soon the prelates wanted to grow their own tea plants, and the Buddhist monk Gyoki dedicated his life to the building of forty-nine temples which he surrounded with tea shrubs brought from China.

This marks the first recorded cultivation of Japanese tea. Other Buddhist priests, returning from studies in China, attempted to plant tea in Japan and were exceedingly successful.

In 805 A.D. Saicho, known posthumously as Dengyo Daishi, brought seeds back from China. He planted them on the site of the present-day tea garden of Ikegami.

In 806 A.D. Kobo Daishi, another Buddhist monk of great reknown, returned from China bringing a quantity of tea seeds with him as well as an intimate and thorough knowledge of tea manufacture.

In 815 A.D. Abbot Yeichu introduced the beverage to Emperor Saga. The monarch immediately decreed that the plant be cultivated by the citizens of the five provinces surrounding his capital. He commanded further that an annual tribute of the leaf for his personal use and for the use of the Imperial Household be levied against these implantations.

The tea drink gained in popularity, but its progress as a beverage and as an article of trade suffered a two-hundred-year setback during the epoch of Japanese civil wars.

With the return of peace, tea drinking and tea cultivation were revived in the year 1191 A.D. by Abbot Yeisai, chief of the Zen sect. Yeisai regarded the tea plant as the source of sacred remedy and he wrote a book on the subject entitled *Kitcha-Yojoki*—"Book of Tea Sanitation." He treated the ills of the mighty Minamoto Shogun Sanetomo, who became a devotee of tea and heralded its fame as a healing agent far and wide. Tea drinking became socially important, and its snob appeal was enhanced by the appearance of the first handsome tea service. Made with a special glaze which was imported from China, the tea set was designed by the very skillful craftsman Toshiro. It set the pattern for the exquisite tea sets which became the vogue. Previously reserved for priests and nobles, tea became the preferred beverage of the masses who were eager to follow the lead of the holy and highborn.

Finally in 1738 Soichiro Nagatani (San-no-jo) invented the process of green-tea manufacture. The newfound technique stimulated the propagation of tea throughout Japan. The legendary past of tea came to a halt with this mercantile discovery; its commercial present—the days of vast tea trade—had begun.

TEA TRAVELS TO
EUROPE AND AMERICA

The legends of tea and tea drinking were firmly established in the Orient for countless centuries before the great custom of tea drinking was introduced to Europe by intrepid Portuguese sailors. Following Vasco da Gama's discovery of an all-sea route to the Indies in 1497, these brave and hearty seamen pushed on to other discoveries which offered them favorable opportunities for trade in silk and spices. When the Portuguese, in their role as the first Europeans to reach the Orient by sea, landed in China, they were regarded by the populace with suspicion. Soon, however, the Chinese understood that the seamen came only to barter and exchange, not to conquer. As a result, the Portuguese enjoyed control of the Oriental spice trade until 1596.

The Portuguese sea lanes opened the way for other ambitious merchants and for missionaries. The earliest European accounts of tea and tea drinking are found in a book entitled *Voyages and Travels*, a collection of sea-faring tales published in Venice by Giambattista Ramusio around 1559. In this work the great Persian merchant Hajji Mohammed is quoted on the subject of a "highly esteemed medicinal decoction made by the Chinese from an herb growing in the district of Szechwan called *chai-catai*."

During these infant years of European commerce with China and Japan, Jesuit missionaries became acquainted with tea, which they called *ch'a* in the detailed accounts of tea drinking, tea plants, and medicinal properties of the beverage which they wrote home. These narratives inspired other courageous fortune-hunting seamen from countries other than Portugal to visit the Far East. Soon the Dutch came to Lisbon to trade for the rich cargo of tea which they in turn transported to France, the Netherlands, and the countries along the Baltic. In 1596, Jan Hugo van Linschooten, a Dutchman who had sailed to the Indies with the Portuguese, wrote an account of his travels which made other Dutch merchants hunger after the rich profits of the Oriental trade.

Sensitive to the mushrooming competition, the Portuguese closed their harbors to the Dutch. Thereupon these stalwarts sent four ships under their own flag to Java, where they established a depot for import and export of Oriental specialties including *ch'a*. Following the Amoy dialect, the Dutch romanized the word to *thee*, setting the pattern for its Western pronunciation which has varied only to a slight degree during all the ensuing centuries.

By 1602 more than sixty-five Dutch vessels had completed the Oriental voyage. Competition among the Dutch became so ruinous that the Crown was forced to charter the Dutch East India Company to unite the rival factions and ameliorate the conflicts. Thus the rich benefits accruing to the Netherlands government from the Indies grubstake were protected. This concord made it possible for the Dutch East India Company to wrest the mastery of the rich spice trade from the Portuguese, a position of dominance which they were successful in maintaining until the turn of the seventeenth century. Then, another greedy giant usurped its monopoly—the English East India Company, chartered in 1600 by Queen Elizabeth I. It was destined to build great fortunes and extend the fingers of its control of the tea trade with powers usually granted only to governments.

The corporation was empowered to make bylaws, export all kinds of goods free of duty, and export foreign coin or bullion. It was permitted to take out of the country coin of the realm (ordinarily prohibited), inflict punishments, impose fines, and enjoy the sole right of trade with the East Indies. With these powers it was able to usurp practically all of the wealth to be found in commerce or discovery between Cape Horn in the Western Hemisphere and the Cape of Good Hope in the Eastern Hemisphere. Simultaneously this monopoly gave rise to the unwholesome competition which brought bands of cutthroats and smugglers to the seas. The journey from the Orient to Europe became perilous. Only the most daring survived.

Although the efforts of the English East India Company contributed much to the growing favor of tea drinking in Europe, the English were slow in becoming tea drinkers. The advertising campaign waged by the noted London coffeehouse keeper Thomas Garway did much to make the Oriental specialty popular. Garway circulated large posters around the city of London offering tea as a novelty at interesting prices. About the same time, Catherine of Braganza, wife of King Charles II, made tea drinking fashionable in court circles by insisting on its use in place of the wines and strong liquors prevalent in that era. From the court the new fad of tea drinking quickly spread to other persons among the well-to-do. In 1710, tea imports totaled eight hundred thousand pounds, and so avid did the English become in their tea drinking that by 1775, less than fifty years later, four million pounds of tea were utilized. Tea was firmly entrenched as the national drink. Hostesses competed for the honor of having the most desirable "social afternoon tea." Beautiful tea sets were designed and executed during the period. Magnificent examples of these are now found in the Lipton Collection of Antique English Silver Related to Tea Drinking, in the Victoria and Albert Museum in London, and in many museums in America.

Soon teas were served in every one of England's famous coffeehouses. Private clubs were founded which specialized in serving tea. As an outgrowth of its popularity the government of Charles II decided to impose the first English tea taxes to compensate for the declining revenues derived from the sale of beer and wine. Attempting to circumvent these taxes, the English established out-of-the-country contacts to get their precious tea, and smuggling became so effectively rampant that at the end of the seventeenth century and for most of the eighteenth century more than half of all the tea drunk in England was brought into the country illegally.

Early settlers in America knew nothing of this ardent English tea drinking, and it is most probable that the joys of this "vice" were introduced to the colonies by the burghers of New Amsterdam. William Penn introduced tea drinking to the Quaker colony which he founded in Delaware in 1682. By the middle of the eighteenth century American colonists were as great consumers of tea as the English. The American reaction to the obnoxious Stamp Act and the events of the American Revolution are too well known to be repeated here, but it is significant that even though Dutch tea smuggling to England and America was on the increase, the English East India Company survived the War of Independence, muddled through its financial difficulties, and emerged more powerful than ever.

Perhaps this was true because of the high caliber of the men who were in the employ of this great commercial enterprise. The most capable generals and captains of the sea served the company in Java, India, China, and other depots overseas. At home in England the directors of the East India Company owed their success to their astute judgment in surrounding themselves with people cleverer than they. On the employment rolls of the company there were such men as Charles Lamb (1775–1834), essayist, humorist, and critic, author of the *Essays of Elia*, who worked almost his whole life long as a clerk in the offices; James Mill (1773–1836), journalist, historian, and political economist, occupied in the company's department of examiners; his son, the celebrated John Stuart Mill (1806–73), philosopher and economist;

Thomas Love Peacock (1785–1866), satirical poet and novelist; and many other distinguished men of letters.

The company faced one jealous outcry after another. When in 1823 tea was discovered to be indigenous to Assam, India, the tea trade of China began its downward trend. Ten years later, however, the East India Company, despite initial reverses, had succeeded in bringing the country of India into subjugation to its vast business interests, which included their interests in the tea industry. All of the administrative functions of this immense land were directed from England, and not until the Indian Mutiny of 1858 did two hundred and fifty-eight years of continuous profits end for the English East India Company—the greatest monopoly of all time.

At the abolition of the monopoly, and in order to meet the competition which had sprung up around them, tea merchants began to demand more rapid transport for each new season's leaf. "The East India Men," frigate ships used to transport the teas, became obsolete. Shipping companies started the search for a swifter means of covering the great distance between the Orient and the European tea centers which developed. American shipbuilders, aware of this demand for speed, started to experiment with a new type of schooner which could attain the speed of the "Baltimore clippers," two-masted beauties created for use in the War of 1812. Considered the fastest sailing ships on the seven seas, the Baltimore clippers helped to usher in the exciting, adventurous era of the tea clippers and inspired the sharply competitive tea races that stirred the blood of the romantic and the mercantile alike. The efficiency of these ships contributed greatly to the economic rise of America and succeeded in giving the merchant seamen of the newest of all nations mastery of the oceans.

In 1832 a Baltimore merchant, Isaac McKim, conceived of having built for the tea trade a three-masted full-rigged ship along the lines of the two-masted Baltimore clipper. The ship, named for his wife, Ann McKim, was decked out with the most handsome fittings that could be found, but though her speed caused a sensation, she could carry only a small crew and cargo. She was, however, the first of the China clippers.

The *Ann McKim* inspired a dreamy-eyed American ship-builder and draftsman named John Willis Griffiths to create the famous *Rainbow*, first of the "extreme" (less blunt and full-bodied) tea clippers. On her first voyage she paid for her cost two times over, and on her second trip she made the tour to China and back in one hundred and eighty days (faster than other ships of the period could sail one way).

Griffiths' genius flowered. His second ship, the *Sea Witch*, was considered the fastest ship in the world, a position it held for three years. American tea merchants, taking note of the new supremacy of American-designed ships, began to commission fleets of their own. In addition to the *Ann McKim*, the *Rainbow*, and the *Sea Witch*, the great tea merchants Howland and Aspinwall owned the *Natchez*. Grinnell, Minturn & Company owned the *Flying Cloud*, *North Wind*, *Sea Serpent*, *Sweepstakes*, and *Sovereign of the Seas*. N. L. & G. Griswold owned the *George Griswold*, *Helena*, *Ariel*, *Panama*, *Tarolinta*, and *Challenge*, which was known in its day as the finest and most costly merchant ship in the world.

Competition between the two flags of Great Britain and America grew keener. Britain answered the clipper-ship challenge of speed with the *Stornoway*, *Torrington*, and *Lord of the Isles*. But the greatest American fleet for the tea trade was owned by A. A. Low & Brother, with their *Houqua*, *Samuel Russell*, *N. B. Palmer*, *Great Republic*, *Yokohama*, and *Oriental*—the first American ship to carry a cargo of tea directly from China to London after the repeal of the prohibitionary English navigation laws.

With the advent of British free trade and the shock of the fact that the *Oriental* was able to make the trip from Canton to London in only ninety-seven days while carrying a cargo as heavy as 1118 tons of tea, the contest for the designing, building, and sailing of even faster ships for the annual tea races grew more heated. It was the practice for seven or eight top-quality ships to leave the Canton River at about the same time and enter the hundred-day race for the profit and honor of being the first ship to arrive in London with a load of tea. The Americans held a marked superiority with the clipper ships designed by Donald McKay. His wondrous ship *Flying Cloud*, a California clipper, accomplished the run around the Horn to San Francisco in eighty-nine days, eight hours—a sailing record that has never been equaled.

The British began building tea clippers in earnest. Their craftsmanship culminated in 1866 in the most famous of all tea races in which the *Ariel* and *Taeping*, both built by Robert Steel & Co. of Greenock, Scotland, reached London in a dead heat after a sail of ninety-nine days. While the *Ariel* had a small lead coming for the finish, the *Taeping* managed to get a faster tug and docked a few minutes earlier. A less satisfactory finish could hardly have been envisioned. Prize and premium money were split—a small consolation for the two great rivals.

For a few years more these exciting tea races were the major news and sporting events of the greatest period of tea-merchandising history, but the advent of steam and the opening of the Suez Canal in 1869 combined to bring to an end the glorious flamboyance of the tea clippers.

Shortly thereafter the foundations of the modern tea industry were laid. The huge tea estates of India, Ceylon, Pakistan, and Indonesia were established. Large-scale production, using the most up-to-date methods, started to provide the world with the highest possible quality in teas.

Since the first pound of tea reached American shores three hundred years ago our own tea industry has grown to such an extent that presently it employs thousands of people and represents millions of dollars. America imports over a hundred thirty million pounds of tea each year to quench the thirst of its faithful tea drinkers.

FROM TEA GARDEN TO TEACUP

Four thousand years have passed since Emperor Shen Nung discovered tea and in the intervening years tea has been most important in the economic structure of the world. For many, many years following the "tea parties" in Boston, Philadelphia, Charleston, and New York, Americans held a strong antipathy to tea and tea drinking. Most assuredly they boycotted tea after the Revolution. Yet today we know Americans to be second only to the British as importers in the tea commerce of the world.

Ninety-seven per cent of the tea Americans drink is *black tea*, grown mainly in India and Ceylon. The remaining small percentage is comprised of *green tea*, grown in Japan, and *oolong tea*, grown in Taiwan. *The difference between black, green, and oolong tea depends only upon the way in which the leaves have been processed after they have been picked, not upon the kind of bush from which the tea has been taken nor upon the country or region in which the tea has been cultivated.*

The teas we purchase are blends. Each one is made from twenty or thirty varieties chosen from the more than three thousand different kinds of tea leaves which are named for the districts in which they are grown. Expert tea tasters utilize their unique skill to judge the tea varieties on such characteristics as color, flavor, bouquet, and body. They combine the tea leaves in such a way that tea manufacturers can reproduce the blend over and over again in order to give the consumer the kind of tea she will want to purchase on a regular basis.

The little dried leaves we tuck away so neatly on our kitchen shelves all come from an evergreen plant in the camellia family. Growing wild at the meeting place of Tibet, India, China, Burma, and Thailand, it is commercially cultivated to the greatest extent in India, Ceylon, Indonesia, Pakistan, Japan, Formosa, Transcaucasia in the USSR, and certain parts of Africa.

Teas of the finest quality grow best at latitudes of three thousand to seven thousand feet above sea level, but they grow more slowly, give smaller yield, and are rarer and more expensive than other teas. Teas from Assam, which is low-lying, prove a singular exception to this rule.

In its natural habitat tea is a jungle plant, but most of the teas we drink are nurtured in the tea gardens of northern India or on the tea estates of southern India, East Africa, Ceylon, and Indonesia. These plantations may stretch from three hundred to three thousand acres. Many of them are completely self-contained, fully equipped with factories, storehouses, lodgings for workers, schools, and hospitals.

At planting time the seeds of the tea plant are laid out six inches apart and nursed until they are from six to eighteen months old. Then they are ready for removal to the tea garden. Careful workers transplant the tea seedlings three to five feet apart in the rich tropical soil of the garden at the rate of about three thousand seedlings per acre. Ferns are used to cover the young plants and protect them from the torrid rays of the sun. When the tea plant grows in the wilderness, it can achieve a height of thirty feet, but in the tea garden these bright evergreens are kept pruned to a height of only three or four feet. This pruning keeps the leaves delicate and tender and makes it easy for the plant to be plucked. When the tree is from three to five years old, new shoots or "flushes" blossom which indicate that the tree is mature enough for harvesting. Each flush produces two tender green leaves and a small unopened bud. This is the part of the tea plant which is used for the tea we drink. These two tiny leaves and the bud are plucked from the bush by hand. Usually no other leaves are taken from the tree. In hot climates the bushes may sprout and be ready for plucking again every seven or eight days, but in tea gardens of the cooler climates the flushing may not take place any more often than every fourteen to sixteen days.

At harvesttime the workers move quickly through the garden. With quick, deft fingers they choose the leaves to be plucked, break them off between thumb and forefinger, and toss them into large baskets which they have tied to their backs or balanced on their heads. An experienced plucker can pick up to sixty pounds of green leaves a day, enough to make twelve pounds of tea leaves or two thousand four hundred cups. (A pound of loose tea will make about two hundred cups, and next to water that makes tea the most popular and least expensive beverage in the whole world.)

After the leaves are plucked the harvest is picked over for stalks and then weighed. In the manufacture of black tea the fresh leaves are sent to the "withering" lofts and spread evenly on racks. Currents of warm air remove the moisture from the leaves. The withering process takes from twelve to twenty-four hours, after which the limp leaves are rolled in special machines to break up the cells and thereby hasten the fermentation process.

The leaves change color during the rolling and begin to give off the fragrant aroma which identifies tea. When the rolling process is completed, the leaves go into cool, humid rooms where they are spread thinly on racks for about two hours. During this time they ferment and turn the color of bright copper pennies. Next, they are placed on trays in a drying machine. Hot dry air is forced into a chamber through which the tea leaves travel. Fermentation is brought to a halt and the leaves dry completely. They seem to be black in color. The tea is graded by size and the leaves are classified as large or small, broken or unbroken. The familiar words "pekoe"

27

(pronounced *peck'-o*), "orange pekoe," and "Souchong" refer only to the *size* of the leaves and *not* to the variety or quality of the tea. The strength of the tea cannot be decided by its color, as some tea leaves naturally develop into a beverage which is light even at full strength. This tea-manufacturing process applies to the making of black teas only. In the manufacture of green tea the seedlings are planted and the trees are pruned and plucked in the same manner as are the black teas. However, *green leaves are not subjected to the withering process nor are they permitted to ferment.* The tender green tea leaves taken from the tea garden go instead to a "steamer," where they are heated to 160° F. The tea leaves turn soft and pliable and are alternately rolled and fired until they are too crisp for further treatment. They remain green.

Oolong teas, on the other hand, are semifermented. After the planting, pruning, and plucking, the oolong tea leaves are slightly fermented by withering for a short period in the sun. Then the leaves are manipulated by hand so that the cells of the leaves are broken down in such a way as to permit only a certain degree of fermentation. Following this adroit maneuver the oolong tea leaves are alternately rolled and fired before being shipped to a central factory where they are fired once again and finally packed for shipment.

After the tea, whether black, green, or oolong, is sorted according to size, it is packed in aluminum-lined, moisture-proof plywood chests for shipment to the great tea markets and auction centers of the world: London, Calcutta and Cochin in India, Chittagong in Pakistan, Colombo in Ceylon, and Nairobi in Kenya. The price of the tea we drink is determined at one of these auctions, and the tea comes to us either directly from one of the centers or indirectly through London.

Before an auction takes place the tea chests, each holding a little more than a hundred pounds of tea, are arranged in long rows in the warehouses. A small hole is bored in each chest which permits a sample of the tea it contains to be extracted. These samples are sent to leading tea buyers around the globe. If the buyer likes a particular sample, he bids on it. As much as sixteen million pounds of tea may be sold at auction during one day. The buyer making the highest bid naturally gets the tea and he ships it directly to a U.S. port serving one of his principals' plants. It may also be shipped to one of his customers to fill an already existing order or he may send samples to importers who are his customers in various parts of the world. Most of the American tea importers who purchase directly from auction are located in the major tea centers of our country: New York, Boston, Philadelphia, Chicago, New Orleans, Los Angeles, San Francisco, and Seattle. These American importers test samples of the tea taken from the chests and place their orders. When the tea chests arrive in the principal U.S. ports of entry they are placed in bonded warehouses. The tea cannot be moved from the warehouse until it has been approved for entry by Tea Examiners employed by the U.S. Food and Drug Administration, which is responsible for the high standards to which the tea we drink is submitted. Teas which do not meet these standards are not admitted into the country under any circumstance. Few other countries of the world enjoy teas of higher quality than those we drink in the United States.

At the offices of the great tea companies, tea tasters perform their discriminating task of choosing perfect blends of tea. The chosen leaves are poured into revolving drums with a capacity of three thousand pounds. These drums mix the tea leaves, which are then automatically packed by great machines that measure the exact amount of tea necessary for each package or tea bag.

The voyage from tea garden to teacup is a long one, but at the end of the trip there await the American tea enthusiasts who annually make and consume more than thirty billion cups of tea, either hot or iced, according to particular inclination and season of the year, at a cost of only about one cent per cup.

COOKING AND BAKING WITH TEA

SAVORY TEA POT ROAST

3- to 4-pound boneless
chuck or round roast
2 teaspoons salt
2 tablespoons vegetable
shortening
4 cups strong tea includ-
ing leaves*

1 bottle (8 ounces) Rus-
sian dressing
¼ cup dark brown sugar
¼ cup lemon juice
2 medium onions, grated

Sprinkle meat with salt. In Dutch oven or heavy saucepan, heat shortening and brown meat on all sides. Pour on tea with leaves; then simmer, covered, 2½ to 3 hours, or until tender, turning meat occasionally.

Remove meat to serving platter; keep warm. Skim off fat; strain broth, reserving 1 cup.

In medium saucepan, combine reserved broth with Russian dressing, brown sugar, lemon juice, and onions. Cook, uncovered, 10 minutes, or until slightly thickened. Serve with roast.

Makes 6 to 8 servings.

* ¼ cup loose tea brewed 5 minutes in 4 cups boiling water

TEA-ORANGE-GLAZED DUCKLING

5- to 6-pound ready-to-
   cook duckling
1 cup strong tea*
¼ cup honey

2 tablespoons soy sauce
2 medium oranges,
   sectioned
2 oranges, halved

Place duckling in roasting pan, then roast in a 350° F. oven for 1½ hours. Drain off fat.

Increase oven temperature to 425° F. Combine tea with honey, soy sauce, and orange sections. Pour over duckling.

Roast, surrounded by orange halves, 50 to 60 minutes longer, or until done, basting occasionally with tea-honey mixture. Remove to serving platter.

Makes 4 servings.

* 2 individual-size tea bags brewed 5 minutes in 1 cup boiling water

TEA-APRICOT-GLAZED HAM STEAK

1 teaspoon instant tea
1 tablespoon water
1 teaspoon lemon juice
¼ cup apricot preserves

1 fully cooked ham steak
   (¾ to 1 inch thick),
   about 1½ pounds

Preheat broiler. Combine instant tea with water, then stir in lemon juice and apricot preserves.

Place ham on broiler rack and spread with part of glaze. Broil about 15 minutes, turning once and basting with remaining glaze. Serve with pan juices.

Makes 3 to 4 servings.

ORIENTAL TEA-HONEY SPARERIBS

2 pounds spareribs   ¼ cup soy sauce
1 cup strong tea*   ½ cup honey

Place spareribs in shallow baking pan; cover and bake in a 425° F. oven one hour. Pour off fat; cut into rib pieces. Increase oven temperature to 450° F.

Combine tea with soy sauce and honey. Pour over spareribs and bake, uncovered, basting occasionally, 30 to 40 minutes, or until crispy brown and tender. Remove to serving platter.

Makes 4 servings.

* 2 individual-size tea bags brewed 5 minutes in 1 cup boiling water

TEA-GLAZED LOIN OF PORK

3- to 4-pound loin of pork   2 tablespoons lemon juice
Salt   ½ cup light corn syrup
1 tablespoon instant tea

Place roast in a shallow roasting pan and sprinkle with salt. Insert roast-meat thermometer in center of meat. Roast in a 325° F. oven for 2 hours; drain off fat.

Increase oven temperature to 400° F. In small saucepan, dissolve instant tea in lemon juice; stir in ½ teaspoon salt and corn syrup. Bring to boil and simmer 1 minute. Spoon some tea syrup over meat and roast ½ hour or until roast-meat thermometer reads 185° F., basting frequently with remaining tea syrup.

Makes 6 to 8 servings.

INSTANT TEA BASTING SAUCE FOR BROILED CHICKEN

1 cup strong tea (use heaping teaspoonful of instant tea)
¼ cup soy sauce
⅓ cup honey

Mix and stir above ingredients together until well blended. Spoon over chicken every few minutes while broiling.

FRUITY PORK CHOPS

4 medium pork chops, about 1½ pounds
1 tablespoon instant tea
Water
1 teaspoon salt
1½ cups mixed dried fruit
1 tablespoon cornstarch

In large skillet brown chops well. Dissolve instant tea in 2 cups water. Pour over chops, add salt and fruit.

Simmer, covered, 50 to 60 minutes, or until meat and fruit are tender. Combine cornstarch with 2 tablespoons water, stir into gravy in skillet; cook until thickened.

Makes 4 servings.

PUMPKIN TEA CHIFFON PIE

2 tablespoons instant tea
¾ cup milk
3 slightly beaten egg yolks
¾ cup light brown sugar
1 envelope unflavored
    gelatine
½ teaspoon salt

1½ teaspoons pumpkin
    pie spice
1¼ cups mashed cooked
    or canned pumpkin
3 egg whites
⅓ cup granulated sugar
1 9-inch baked pastry
    shell

In small saucepan, dissolve instant tea in milk; then blend in egg yolks, brown sugar, gelatine, salt, and pumpkin pie spice. Bring to a boil over low heat, stirring constantly. Remove from heat and stir in pumpkin. Refrigerate until cool, about 1 hour.

In medium bowl, beat egg whites until soft peaks form; gradually add granulated sugar, beating until stiff.

Fold pumpkin mixture thoroughly into egg whites. Turn into pastry shell and chill until firm.

If desired, garnish with a border of whipped cream and sprinkle with toasted slivered almonds, chopped walnuts, or pecans.

Makes 8 servings.

TEA PIE

1 baked 9-inch pastry
  shell
1½ cups sugar
⅓ cup cornstarch
2 tablespoons instant tea
1¾ cups water

3 egg yolks, beaten
3 tablespoons butter
3 egg whites
¼ teaspoon cream of
  tartar
6 tablespoons sugar

Mix 1½ cups sugar and cornstarch in saucepan; disolve instant tea in water and stir into sugar mixture.

Place over medium heat and cook, stirring constantly, until mixture thickens and boils. Boil, still stirring, 1 minute longer.

Slowly stir half the hot mixture into beaten egg yolks, then blend with remaining hot mixture in saucepan. Continue boiling 1 minute longer, stirring constantly. Remove from heat and blend in butter. Turn into pie shell.

Beat egg whites and cream of tartar until frothy. Beat in 6 tablespoons sugar gradually; continue beating until very stiff and glossy. Pile meringue on filling and seal to edges of pastry. Bake in a 350° F. oven about 15 minutes, or until top is golden brown. Cool in slightly warm spot, away from drafts.

Makes 6 to 8 servings.

MARBLED TEA LOAVES

1 package (2-layer) yellow cake mix
3 tablespoons instant tea
1 tablespoon milk

Grease and flour 2 1½-quart loaf pans. Prepare cake mix as label directs. In medium bowl, dissolve instant tea in milk and blend in half of batter.

Spoon plain and tea mixtures alternately into prepared pans. With spatula or knife, cut through batter in wide zigzag to give marbled effect. Bake in a 350° F. oven about 45 minutes or until cake tests done. Cool on racks.

Makes 2 loaves.

TEA FRUITCAKE

½ pound butter or margarine
2½ cups granulated sugar
1 teaspoon pure vanilla extract
1 teaspoon lemon extract
1 can (3½ ounces) flaked coconut
1½ cups mixed glacé fruits
1½ cups seedless raisins
1 jar (4 ounces) candied orange peel
1 cup walnut halves

1 cup pecan halves
1 cup slivered blanched almonds
½ cup honey
2¾ cups sifted all-purpose flour
1½ teaspoons double-acting baking powder
1 teaspoon salt
1 cup milk
½ cup instant tea
6 egg whites
About 12 candied cherries

In kettle or other large container, with mixer at medium speed, beat butter or margarine with sugar until creamy, then blend in vanilla and lemon extracts. With wooden spoon, mix in coconut, glacé fruits, raisins, candied orange peel, walnuts, pecans, almonds, and honey; mix well.

Sift flour with baking powder and salt. Gradually stir milk into instant tea; add alternately with flour mixture to fruit mixture, blending well. Beat egg whites until stiff, then fold into fruit-nut mixture.

Fill 2 well-greased 10x3½x2½-inch straight-sided loaf and dessert pans with mixture. Arrange candied cherries on top of batter.

Bake in a 300° F. oven about 2 hours, or until cake tester inserted in center comes out clean.

Cool completely on wire racks. Loosen edges and turn out of pans, then wrap in foil. Cakes keep several months in refrigerator.

Makes 2 loaves.

APRICOT TEA UPSIDE-DOWN CAKE

¼ cup butter or margarine
½ cup light brown sugar
1 tablespoon instant tea
1 teaspoon water

1 can (1 pound) apricot
halves, drained
6 cooked prunes, pitted
1 package (2-layer)
yellow cake mix

Grease a 9-inch piepan and a 9-inch layer cake pan. In small saucepan, melt butter or margarine and add brown sugar. Combine instant tea with water and stir into sugar mixture until sugar is melted.

Spread tea-sugar mixture in bottom of the piepan, and on it arrange apricots, cut side up, with prunes.

Prepare cake mix as package directs, pouring half of batter over fruit and remaining batter in the layer cake pan. Bake in a 350° F. oven about 35 minutes or until cakes test done. Cool extra layer and store for future use.

Invert apricot tea cake immediately onto a cake plate. Serve warm; top with whipped cream if desired.

Makes 8 servings.

MARBLED TEA PUNCH CAKE

1 package (2-layer)
   yellow cake mix
2 envelopes unflavored
   gelatine
2 cups cranberry juice
   cocktail
Water

1 can (6 ounces) frozen
   limeade concentrate,
   thawed
3 tablespoons instant tea
2 tablespoons lemon juice
1 large banana, thinly
   sliced (optional)

Prepare cake mix according to package directions using 2 8x8x2-inch baking pans. Cool one on rack and freeze for future use. Leave other in pan for Marbled Tea Punch Cake.

In small saucepan, dissolve gelatine in 1 cup cranberry juice cocktail over low heat while stirring until dissolved. In a quart measure, add water to limeade concentrate to make 2 cups liquid. Stir in instant tea, 1 cup cranberry juice cocktail, and lemon juice. Then add gelatine mixture. Chill in refrigerator until mixture is syrupy.

With a two-tined fork pierce cake to bottom, making large holes in rows ½ inch apart. Slowly spoon half of tea-gelatine mixture over cake, allowing liquid to seep down through holes. Refrigerate cake and remaining tea-gelatine mixture until gelatine is thickened, then spoon half of remaining mixture over the cake and arrange banana slices on top. Spoon rest of mixture over fruit to glaze top. If desired, garnish with flaked coconut and/or whipped cream.

LEMON TEA CAKE

1 package lemon spongecake
¼ cup instant tea

Make cake according to package directions, blending instant tea into the batter. Bake in round or square angel-cake pan. After cake is cooled, spread top and sides with Lemon Tea Glaze.

LEMON TEA GLAZE

1 teaspoon grated lemon
   rind
¼ cup lemon juice
2 egg yolks, beaten

2 tablespoons softened
   butter or margarine
3 to 3½ cups sifted
   confectioners' sugar
1 tablespoon instant tea

Grate lemon rind. Squeeze lemon or lemons for juice and add grated rind to extract more flavor.

Stir egg yolks into butter or margarine. Add lemon juice and rind alternately with sugar. Stir in instant tea.

TEA LEMON CAKE

1 package (2-layer)
   yellow cake mix
1 cup butter or margarine
4 cups sifted confec-
   tioners' sugar

¼ cup instant tea
¼ cup water
1 tablespoon grated
   lemon rind

Bake cake mix following package directions in a 13x9x2-inch baking pan.

In mixer bowl, beat butter or margarine and 1 cup confectioners' sugar until blended. Dissolve instant tea in water, then add alternately with remaining confectioners' sugar to butter mixture; beat well. Stir in lemon rind.

When cake is cool, split cake to form 2 layers. Use tea-butter frosting to fill and frost cake. Decorate with lemon twists if desired. Cut into desired shape and size.

Makes about 15 servings.

TEA CAKE RING

1 cup soft butter or margarine	1 teaspoon pure vanilla extract
1 cup granulated sugar	3 cups sifted cake flour
1 cup sifted confectioners' sugar	2 teaspoons double-acting baking powder
6 egg yolks	1 cup milk
2 tablespoons grated lemon rind	2 tablespoons instant tea
	6 egg whites

In large bowl, with mixer at medium speed, beat butter or margarine until creamy; gradually beat in sugars until creamy. Then gradually add egg yolks and beat until very light and fluffy, about 7 minutes. Add lemon rind and vanilla extract.

In small bowl, sift together flour and baking powder. Gradually stir milk into instant tea. At low speed, blend in flour-mixture alternately with tea-milk, in three parts, starting and ending with flour.

In small bowl, beat egg whites until stiff but not dry; then carefully fold into batter. Turn into greased 3-quart bundt pan or 10-inch tube pan and bake in a 350° F. oven 1 hour or until cake tester inserted in center comes out clean. Cool on rack in pan 10 minutes, then invert cake on rack; remove pan and cool.

Makes about 20 slices.

TEA CAKE LOAVES

1 *cup soft butter or margarine*	1 *teaspoon pure vanilla extract*
1 *cup granulated sugar*	3 *cups sifted cake flour*
1 *cup sifted confectioners' sugar*	2 *teaspoons double-acting baking powder*
6 *egg yolks*	1 *cup milk*
2 *tablespoons grated lemon rind*	2 *tablespoons instant tea*
	6 *egg whites*

In large bowl, with mixer at medium speed, beat butter or margarine until creamy; gradually beat in sugars until creamy. Then gradually add egg yolks and beat until very light and fluffy, about 7 minutes. Add lemon rind and vanilla extract.

In small bowl, sift together flour and baking powder. Gradually stir milk into instant tea.

At low speed, blend in flour-mixture alternately with tea-milk in 3 parts, starting and ending with flour.

In small bowl, beat egg whites until stiff but not dry; carefully fold into batter. Turn into 2 greased 8½x4½x2½-inch foil loaf pans and bake in a 350° F. oven 1 hour or until cake tester inserted in center comes out clean.

Cool on rack in pans 10 minutes, then invert cakes on rack; remove pans and cool.

Makes 2 loaves.

PINEAPPLE TEA CHEESECAKE

½ cup sifted all-purpose
   flour
Granulated sugar
¼ cup butter or margarine
1 egg yolk
¼ cup plus 1 tablespoon
   instant tea
2 tablespoons milk
3 packages (8 ounces
   each) cream cheese

4 eggs
1 teaspoon pure vanilla
   extract
1 tablespoon grated
   lemon rind
1 can (8¾ ounces)
   crushed pineapple,
   undrained
1 tablespoon cornstarch
1 tablespoon lemon juice

Combine flour with 2 tablespoons sugar; cut in butter or margarine until it resembles coarse cornmeal, then stir in egg yolk. Form into a smooth ball. Refrigerate until chilled, about 1 hour.

Start heating oven to 400° F. Roll dough between floured waxed paper into a 9-inch circle. Remove from waxed paper and place on bottom of 9-inch spring-form pan. Bake about 10 minutes or until golden; cool. Generously grease side of spring-form pan, then flour. Return bottom to spring-form pan. Reduce oven heat to 325° F.

Dissolve ¼ cup instant tea in milk. In medium bowl, with mixer at medium speed, beat cheese until creamy, then add eggs one at a time, gradually adding 1 cup sugar. Beat until smooth and thick, then add vanilla, tea-milk, and lemon rind. Scrape bowl and beater occasionally.

Turn into prepared spring-form pan. Bake about 35 minutes or until set. Turn off heat, open door; let cake stand in oven until cool, about 2 hours. Refrigerate until chilled, then remove side of pan.

In small saucepan blend 1 tablespoon cornstarch with 2

tablespoons sugar, stir in pineapple, and cook while stirring until clear and thickened.

Blend 1 tablespoon instant tea with lemon juice and stir into pineapple mixture. Cool slightly and spoon over top of cake. Garnish with slivered almonds.

Makes about 10 servings.

BREAKFAST TEA RING

1 package active dry yeast	1 jar (4 ounces) candied
¼ cup warm water	orange peel
½ cup milk, scalded	3 cups sifted all-purpose
Granulated sugar	flour
1 teaspoon salt	¼ cup instant tea
Butter or margarine	¾ cup chopped pecans
1 egg, beaten	

In measuring cup, sprinkle yeast onto warm water. Stir to dissolve. In large bowl, combine hot milk, ¼ cup sugar, salt, and ¼ cup butter or margarine. Cool until lukewarm, then stir in egg, dissolved yeast, and orange peel.

Stir in 1 cup flour, then remaining flour; beat until smooth and elastic. Place in greased bowl, cover and let rise in warm place (80° to 85° F.) until double in bulk—about 1½ hours. Punch dough down; then roll out on well-floured board into a 18x12-inch rectangle. Brush with 2 tablespoons melted butter or margarine. Combine 6 tablespoons sugar with instant tea. Sprinkle over dough, then sprinkle with pecans. Roll lengthwise as for jelly roll, form into a ring, pinching ends together and placing on greased baking sheet.

With scissors snip top—at about 1-inch intervals. Cover and let rise in warm place until double in bulk.

Bake in a 375° F. oven 20 to 30 minutes, or until golden brown. Brush with Tea-Honey Glaze, then cool on rack.

TEA-HONEY GLAZE

2 tablespoons instant tea	¼ cup honey
1 tablespoon water	1 tablespoon butter or margarine

In small saucepan, combine instant tea with water until smooth. Add honey and butter, then bring to boil while stirring. Use to brush tops of hot tea rings.

Makes 1 cake.

CARIBBEAN PUDDING

¼ cup instant tea	½ teaspoon ground cloves
1 cup water	3 eggs, beaten
1 cup seedless raisins	¼ cup butter or margarine, melted
1 cup fine dry bread crumbs	1 cup milk
¾ cup granulated sugar	1 teaspoon rum extract
½ teaspoon salt	1 cup toasted slivered almonds
2 teaspoons ground cinnamon	

In small bowl, combine instant tea with water. Add raisins; cover and plump in refrigerator 2 or 3 days (preferable) or overnight.

In large bowl, combine bread crumbs, sugar, salt, cinnamon, and cloves. Add eggs, butter, milk, and rum extract. Mix until ingredients are well combined. Add almonds and raisin-tea mixture.

Turn mixture into 1-quart casserole. Place in a pan of hot water. Bake in a 350° F. oven 1½ hours. Serve hot with Tea Whipped Cream.

TEA WHIPPED CREAM

In a small bowl, whip ½ cup heavy cream with 1 tablespoon sugar and 2 teaspoons instant tea.

Makes about 6 servings.

TEA APPLE PILLOWS

½ cup butter or margarine
Sifted all-purpose flour
Water
3 tablespoons instant tea
2 teaspoons lemon juice
5 tablespoons granulated sugar
2 tablespoons brown sugar

⅛ teaspoon salt
⅛ teaspoon ground nutmeg
1½ cups finely diced, peeled apples
6 tablespoons sifted confectioners' sugar

Cut butter or margarine into 1½ cups flour until mixture resembles coarse cornmeal. Toss flour mixture with 2 to 3 tablespoons water to form ball.

In medium bowl, blend 2 tablespoons instant tea with lemon juice; add sugars, salt, and nutmeg, blending well. On lightly floured surface, roll out dough ⅛ inch thick; cut into 4-inch squares, rerolling dough as necessary. Place a heaping tablespoon of apples and 1 teaspoon tea-sugar mixture on each square. Moisten edges with water and bring the 4 corners up to the center, pinching the sides well to seal. Continue the same procedure for remaining tarts.

Bake on cookie sheet in a 425° F. oven 25 minutes or until top is golden. Combine confectioners' sugar, 1 tablespoon water, and 1 tablespoon instant tea. Use to glaze top of hot "pillows." Cool on racks.

Makes 12 pillows.

TEA-CREAM-FILLED CUPCAKES

1 *package (2-layer)*	2 *tablespoons instant tea*
yellow cake mix	1 *package vanilla instant*
1½ *cups light cream*	*pudding mix*

Line cupcake pans with paper cupcake liners. Prepare cake mix as label directs; fill pans two thirds full. Bake in a 350° F. oven as label directs. Cool on rack.

In medium bowl, blend cream with instant tea. Add pudding mix and beat as label directs. Chill.

With paring knife, remove cone-shaped piece from top center of each cupcake. Fill each cupcake with about 1 tablespoon of tea-cream. Replace tops.

Makes about 24 medium cupcakes.

TEA-GLAZED PETITS FOURS

1 *baked or packaged*	*Instant tea*
pound cake loaf (about	2 *packages (1 pound)*
13 *ounces)*	*confectioners' sugar,*
Water	*sifted*

Cut pound cake into 3 dozen cubes, about 1½ inches high. Trim, if necessary, for straight sides. Separate and place on racks, over jelly-roll pan, to dry.

Meanwhile, make glaze: In large bowl, combine 6 table-

47

spoons water and 3 tablespoons instant tea. Stir to dissolve. Add 4½ cups sugar and stir until smooth and consistency of a thin frosting (add a few drops more water if needed).

Generously spoon or pour glaze over each cake cube on racks, covering tops and sides evenly. With rubber spatula, scrape drippings from pan and reuse. Allow glaze to dry thoroughly, uncovered, overnight. Repeat process until all cubes are covered. Decorate as desired. Let stand about a day to dry before serving.

Makes about 3 dozen dainty petits fours.

TEA WALNUT TARTLETS

¼ *pound butter or margarine*	¼ *teaspoon salt*
Granulated sugar	½ *cup light cream*
1 *egg*	¼ *cup instant tea*
1¾ *cups all-purpose flour*	2 *cups chopped walnuts*
	2 *tablespoons honey*

In small bowl, with mixer at medium speed, beat butter or margarine and ¼ cup sugar until creamy; add egg. Then with pastry fork blend in flour and salt to form a smooth ball. Refrigerate until thoroughly chilled (several hours).

Stir cream into instant tea. Then in large skillet, over medium heat, melt 1½ cups sugar, stirring constantly, until it forms a golden syrup. Add walnuts, honey, and tea-cream mixture, blending well; set aside.

On lightly floured board, roll out dough ⅛ inch thick. With 2½-inch scalloped pastry cutter cut out about 4 dozen circles and fit into 1¾-inch muffin pan cups. Fill half full with tea-walnut mixture.

Bake in a 375° F. oven 12 to 15 minutes or until golden. Remove from pans to racks.

Makes about 4 dozen tartlets.

TEA-ORANGE GLAZED DUCKLING. Quarters of savory-glazed duckling, roasted and garnished with orange halves, make a festive main course dish for holiday serving.

ED TEA SHERBET. This luscious dessert is bound to play a winning hand at bridge table as well as rate a round of applause at the family dinner table.

AUSTRALIAN TRIFLE. A popular dessert served with tea "down under."

TEA CUPCAKES

¼ pound soft butter or
  margarine
½ cup granulated sugar
1 cup sifted confectioners'
  sugar, divided
2 egg yolks
1 tablespoon grated
  lemon rind
½ teaspoon pure vanilla
  extract
½ cup chopped walnuts

1½ cups sifted cake flour
1 teaspoon double-acting
  baking powder
½ cup milk
2 tablespoons instant tea,
  divided
2 egg whites
1 tablespoon water
Glacéed cherries
Quartered blanched al-
  monds, split

Line about 18 2½-inch muffin pan cups with cupcake papers.

In medium bowl, with mixer at medium speed, beat butter or margarine until creamy, gradually beat in granulated sugar and ½ cup confectioners' sugar until creamy. Then gradually add egg yolks and beat until very light and fluffy, about 7 minutes. Add lemon rind, vanilla extract, and walnuts.

In small bowl, sift together flour and baking powder. Gradually stir milk into 1 tablespoon instant tea. At low speed, blend in flour mixture alternately with tea-milk mixture, in three parts, starting and ending with flour.

In small bowl, beat egg whites until stiff but not dry; then carefully fold into batter. Fill lined muffin cups about two thirds full, bake in a 375° F. oven about 25 minutes, or until cake tester inserted in center comes out clean.

Remove to racks to cool. Combine ½ cup confectioners' sugar, 1 tablespoon instant tea, and water; use to glaze top of Tea Cupcakes. Garnish with glacéed cherries and almonds.

Makes about 18 cupcakes.

TEA WAFERS

⅓ cup butter or margarine
⅔ cup sugar
¼ teaspoon salt
1 egg
3 tablespoons instant tea

1⅓ cups sifted all-purpose flour
¼ teaspoon baking powder

Cream together margarine, sugar, and salt. In a separate bowl, beat egg and tea together until tea is dissolved. Stir into creamed mixture.

Sift together flour and baking powder. Add half the tea mixture. Stir until well blended. Blend in remaining flour.

Refrigerate 3 to 4 hours. Divide dough in half. Refrigerate one half. Roll other half out to ⅛-inch thickness. Cut with cookie cutter into desired shapes. Bake on ungreased baking sheet in a 350° F. oven 8 to 10 minutes.

Repeat with remaining dough.

When cool, frost with a lemon glaze made by blending confectioners' sugar with enough lemon juice to make a spreadable consistency.

Makes 4 dozen wafers.

CHINESE ALMOND COOKIES

1 cup (2 sticks) butter or margarine
1 cup sugar
2 egg yolks
1 teaspoon almond extract

2 cups sifted all-purpose flour
1 cup chopped almonds
Tea Frosting

Cream margarine. Add sugar and beat until light and fluffy. Add egg yolks and almond extract; blend well. Add sifted flour and chopped almonds; mix thoroughly.

Form dough into 1-inch balls. Place balls on ungreased baking sheet. Press down to form cookies ¼ inch thick. Bake in a 325° F. oven 15 minutes.

Cool on wire rack, then spread tops with frosting, topping center of each with a whole almond, if desired.

Makes about 4 dozen cookies.

TEA FROSTING: Dissolve 4 tablespoons instant tea in 2 tablespoons milk. Cream ½ cup (1 stick) butter or margarine until light and fluffy. Add 2½ cups sifted confectioners' sugar and the tea mixture, beating until smooth and creamy.

HAPPY TEA BALLS

About 6 dozen packaged
  vanilla wafers, finely
  crushed (2½ cups
  crumbs)
1 cup confectioners' sugar

1 cup finely chopped
  walnuts
6 tablespoons brandy
2 tablespoons instant tea
3 tablespoons corn syrup
Granulated sugar

In medium bowl, combine vanilla wafer crumbs, confectioners' sugar, and walnuts.

Stir brandy into instant tea; add with corn syrup to crumb mixture, blending well.

Shape into 1-inch balls, then roll them in granulated sugar. Wrap each ball tightly in plastic wrap and store tightly covered to mellow for a few weeks.

Makes about 3½ dozen Happy Tea Balls.

TEA LEAF COOKIES

½ cup butter or margarine
½ cup granulated sugar
1 tablespoon water
2 tablespoons instant tea
1 egg
½ teaspoon salt

1 teaspoon grated lemon rind
½ cup finely chopped walnuts
1½ cups sifted all-purpose flour

In small bowl, with mixer at medium speed, beat butter or margarine and sugar until creamy.

Stir water into instant tea; add to butter mixture with egg, salt, lemon rind, and walnuts, beating until light and fluffy.

Blend in flour, then chill 1 hour. Shape dough into 2 rolls, each about 7 inches long and 1½ inches in diameter. Wrap in foil and chill at least 2 hours, or overnight.

Cut dough into ⅛-inch slices. Place slices on ungreased cookie sheets and shape each with 2 fingers tapering to a point to resemble a leaf; mark veins with blunt edge of table knife. Bake in a 375° F. oven about 10 minutes, or until light brown.

Makes about 7 dozen cookies.

TEA BLONDES

¾ cup sifted all-purpose flour
½ teaspoon double-acting baking powder
2 eggs
1 cup granulated sugar

¼ cup butter or margarine, melted, cooled
2 tablespoons instant tea
1 tablespoon water
½ cup coarsely chopped walnuts

Sift flour and baking powder together. In medium bowl, beat eggs thoroughly; add sugar gradually, beating well. Stir in butter or margarine.

Dissolve instant tea in water, then add to egg mixture. Add flour mixture, blending well; stir in nuts.

Turn into greased 8x8x2-inch pan. Bake in a 350° F. oven 30 to 35 minutes or until top looks dry. Cool in pan. Cut into squares or strips.

SWEET POTATO NUT COOKIES

6 tablespoons instant tea
2 tablespoons milk
½ cup butter or margarine
1½ cups granulated sugar
3 eggs
1 can (1 pound) sweet
   potatoes, drained,
   mashed
½ teaspoon salt

1 tablespoon grated
   lemon rind
½ cup chopped walnuts
1 cup seedless raisins
2½ cups sifted all-purpose
   flour
4 teaspoons double-acting
   baking powder

Dissolve instant tea in milk. In large bowl, with mixer at medium speed, beat butter or margarine and sugar until creamy. Add eggs, sweet potatoes, salt, and tea-milk mixture, then stir in lemon rind, walnuts, and raisins.

Sift together flour and baking powder and blend into tea-sugar mixture.

Drop by teaspoonfuls, 2 inches apart, on greased cookie sheet. Bake in a 375° F. oven 15 to 20 minutes or until golden brown. Cool on rack.

Makes about 4 dozen cookies.

SWISS TEA-NUT SQUARES

1 cup butter or margarine
1 cup granulated sugar
4 eggs, separated
¼ cup instant tea
2 tablespoons milk
1 cup finely ground
  pecans

1 cup sifted all-purpose
  flour
2 teaspoons double-acting
  baking powder
12 pecan halves for gar-
  nish (optional)

In large bowl, with mixer at medium speed, beat butter or margarine with sugar until creamy, then add egg yolks and beat until light and fluffy.

Dissolve instant tea in milk, then add with ground pecans to sugar mixture. Sift together flour and baking powder. Beat egg whites until stiff, then fold alternately with flour, in three parts, into tea-sugar mixture.

Turn into greased 13x9x2-inch baking pan. Arrange pecan halves on top. Bake in a 350° F. oven about 30 minutes, or until cake tests done. Cool on rack, then cut into squares.

Makes 12 large or 24 small squares.

GINGERED TEA SHERBET

⅓ cup loose tea
1 teaspoon dried mint
1⅓ cups boiling water
1 cup ginger ale
1⅔ cups milk
1 cup cream

1½ cups sugar
1 tablespoon grated
  orange rind
½ cup lemon juice
⅛ teaspoon salt

Combine tea and mint leaves in small bowl. Add boiling water. Brew 5 minutes. Strain.

To the tea add ginger ale and enough milk to make 3 cups liquid. Add cream.

Mix together sugar, orange rind, lemon juice, and salt. Slowly add to tea mixture.

Pour into refrigerator trays or 6-cup mold. Freeze until firm. Stir two or three times during freezing period.

Makes about 8 servings.

SPICED TEA SHERBET

⅓ cup loose tea
1 teaspoon dried mint
1⅓ cups boiling water
2⅔ cups milk
1 cup cream
¼ teaspoon ground ginger

¼ teaspoon ground cloves
½ teaspoon ground cinnamon
1½ cups sugar
½ cup lemon juice
⅛ teaspoon salt

Combine tea and mint leaves in small bowl. Add boiling water. Brew 5 minutes. Strain. Add enough milk to make 3 cups liquid. Add cream.

Mix together spices, sugar, lemon juice, and salt. Slowly add to tea mixture.

Pour into refrigerator trays or 6-cup mold. Freeze until firm. Stir two or three times during freezing period.

Makes about 8 servings.

FRUITED TEA SHERBET

1⅓ cups hot double-
  strength tea
1 teaspoon dried mint
1 cup orange juice
1½ cups milk

1 cup cream
1½ cups sugar
½ cup lemon juice
⅛ teaspoon salt
1 cup mashed bananas

Combine tea and mint in bowl; brew 5 minutes. Strain. Add orange juice and enough milk to make 3 cups. Add cream, sugar, lemon juice, salt, and bananas.

Freeze in refrigerator ice trays at coldest temperature until firm. Stir two or three times during freezing time.

Makes 8 to 10 servings.

LEMON TEA SHERBET

2¼ cups strong tea
1 cup sugar
1 envelope unflavored
  gelatine

¼ cup cold water
¼ cup lemon juice
2 egg whites

In small saucepan, combine tea with sugar and boil 10 minutes. Soften gelatine in cold water and stir into hot syrup until gelatine is dissolved. Cool, then stir in lemon juice.

In medium bowl, beat egg whites until stiff but not dry. Gradually fold in tea mixture and pour into 2 refrigerator trays. Freeze until almost firm.

Turn into chilled mixer bowl; beat until light and fluffy, first at low speed, then at high speed. Quickly return to trays, cover with foil, freeze until firm (overnight).

Makes about 6 cups or 12 servings.

BAVARIAN TEA CREAM

⅓ cup sugar
⅛ teaspoon salt
1 envelope unflavored
   gelatine
3 tablespoons instant tea
1¼ cups milk

3 eggs, separated
½ teaspoon pure vanilla
   extract
1 cup heavy cream,
   whipped

Measure sugar into top of a double boiler. Add salt, gelatine, and instant tea. Mix well.

Beat milk and egg yolks together and add gradually to dissolve instant tea. Stir constantly over boiling water until gelatine is completely dissolved, about 5 minutes.

Remove from heat and blend in vanilla. Chill, stirring occasionally, until consistency of unbeaten egg white.

Add egg whites and beat until light and foamy; fold in whipped cream. Pour into a 1-quart mold and chill until firm.*

Unmold on serving platter and garnish individual servings with whipped cream, Amber Tea Sauce, Tea-Sugar Topping. Use a combination of any of these garnishes or "the works"!

Makes 6 servings.

* To make ahead of time, simply pour the cream into individual paper cups or a refrigerator tray and freeze.

AMBER TEA SAUCE

⅔ cup sugar
2 teaspoons instant tea
⅔ cup boiling water

Place sugar in a heavy skillet or saucepan. Stir constantly over medium heat until sugar melts to a light brown syrup.

Meanwhile, dissolve instant tea in boiling water; slowly stir into carmelized sugar. Boil 6 minutes. Cool.

Makes ⅔ cup sauce.

TEA-SUGAR TOPPING

> 2 *tablespoons instant tea*
> ⅓ *cup sugar*

Combine and sprinkle over whipped topping on Bavarian Tea Cream.

Makes approximately ⅓ cup topping.

TEA ICE CREAM WITH TOASTED ALMONDS

> ½ *cup instant tea*
> ¼ *teaspoon allspice*
> 1 *cup water*
> 1 *cup evaporated milk, scalded*
> 3 *eggs, separated*
> 1½ *cups sugar*
>
> ¼ *teaspoon salt*
> 1 *teaspoon lemon juice*
> 2 *teaspoons grated lemon rind*
> 1 *cup heavy cream*
> 1 *cup toasted almonds, chopped*

Combine tea, allspice, water, and scalded milk.

Beat egg yolks, 1 cup sugar, and salt. Add tea mixture and cook over boiling water until thickened, stirring constantly. Cool. Add lemon juice and rind.

Beat egg whites until stiff and beat in remaining sugar. Whip cream until thick enough to hold a soft peak; fold egg whites, whipped cream, and toasted almonds into cooled mixture. Pour into two refrigerator trays.

Freeze until firm.

Makes about 6 to 8 servings.

APRICOT TEA ICE CREAM

½ cup loose tea
½ teaspoon allspice
1 cup boiling water
1 cup evaporated milk,
    scalded
3 eggs, separated
1½ cups sugar

¼ teaspoon salt
1 tablespoon lemon juice
2 teaspoons grated lemon
    rind
1 cup heavy cream
½ cup dried apricots,
    chopped

Combine tea and allspice. Pour boiling water over leaves. Immediately add scalded milk. Brew 5 minutes. Strain. Cool to room temperature.

Beat egg yolks, 1 cup sugar, and salt. Add cooled tea mixture and cook over boiling water until thickened, stirring constantly. Cool. Add lemon juice and rind.

Beat egg whites until stiff and beat in remaining sugar. Whip cream until thick enough to hold a soft peak; fold egg whites and whipped cream into cooled mixture; pour into refrigerator trays or a 6-cup mold.

Stir in apricots when ice cream is half frozen. Freeze until firm.

Makes about 8 servings.

COCONUT TEA ICE CREAM

½ cup loose tea
½ teaspoon allspice
1 cup boiling water
1 cup evaporated milk, scalded
3 eggs, separated
1½ cups sugar

¼ teaspoon salt
1 tablespoon lemon juice
2 teaspoons grated lemon rind
1 cup heavy cream
1 cup coconut, finely chopped

Combine tea and allspice. Pour boiling water over leaves. Immediately add scalded milk. Brew 5 minutes. Strain. Cool to room temperature.

Beat egg yolks, 1 cup sugar, and salt. Add cooled tea mixture and cook over boiling water till thickened, stirring constantly. Cool. Add lemon juice and rind.

Beat egg whites until stiff and beat in remaining sugar. Whip cream until thick enough to hold a soft peak; fold egg whites and whipped cream into cooled mixture; pour into refrigerator trays or a 6-cup mold.

Stir in coconut when ice cream is half frozen. Freeze until firm.

Makes about 8 servings.

QUICK BAVARIAN CREAM

1 package (3 ounces) lemon-lime gelatin dessert
1 cup boiling water

2 tablespoons instant tea
1 cup heavy cream, whipped

Dissolve gelatin dessert in boiling water; stir in instant tea and chill until consistency of unbeaten egg white. Fold in whipped cream and pour into a 4-cup mold. Chill until firm.

When ready to serve, unmold and cut in slices. Garnish with fruit, if desired.

Makes about 6 servings.

TEA-SICLES

3 tablespoons instant tea
2¼ cups water
¾ cup granulated sugar

1 can (6 ounces) frozen
lemonade concentrate,
thawed
Ice pop sticks

Dissolve instant tea in water, stir in sugar until dissolved. Add lemonade concentrate and mix thoroughly.

Pour into ice-pop molds or small paper cups. Freeze nearly firm. Insert a stick upright into the center of each for handle. Freeze firm.

Makes about 12 pops.

TEA DRINKS

SPICED TEA FRUIT CUBES

2 sticks cinnamon,
   2 inches long
8 whole cloves
3 cups boiling water
4 tea bags

1 can (6 ounces) frozen
   lemonade concentrate
Thin lemon slices cut
   into halves or quarters
Maraschino cherries
Mint sprigs

Simmer cinnamon and cloves in boiling water for 5 minutes. Remove from heat, add tea bags, and steep for 5 minutes.

Strain and add lemonade concentrate.

Pour into ice-cube trays. Insert lemon slice, maraschino cherry, or mint sprig into each cube and freeze until solid. Delicious in iced tea or fruit drink.

ORANGE FROSTEA

3 cups of strong tea, cooled
6 tablespoons frozen orange juice
6 scoops orange sherbet

Mix tea, orange juice (just as it comes from container), and sherbet in blender or shaker. Serve in tall glasses.

Makes 6 servings.

SPICED LEMON SYRUP FOR TEA

Juice of 3 lemons
Rind of 1 lemon
Several whole cloves

3 cups sugar
6 sprigs mint

Heat ingredients over low heat and stir until syrup comes to a boil. Strain. Add 1 teaspoon or more to a cup of hot tea.

For iced tea: Add ½ cup boiling water to lemon syrup after straining. Stir 1 teaspoon or more lemon syrup into a glass of iced tea.

LIME DELIGHT

4 cups strong tea, cooled
Juice of 1 lime

3 tablespoons maraschino
  cherry juice
2 tablespoons sugar

Combine all ingredients.
  Pour over ice cubes in tall glass.
  Garnish drink with a twist of lime peel and a cherry.

Makes 4 to 6 servings.

TROPICAL TEA

3 cups tea, cooled
1 can (6 ounces) frozen lemonade concentrate

Combine tea and lemonade concentrate.
  Pour over ice in tall glasses.

Makes 4 servings.

ALMOND-FLAVORED TEA LEMONADE

3 cups strong tea, cooled
1 teaspoon almond flavoring
1 can (6 ounces) frozen lemonade concentrate

Combine ingredients and stir until well blended.
  Pour over ice in tall glasses.

Makes 4 to 6 servings.

TEA LEMONADE

2 quarts tea, cooled
1 can (6 ounces) frozen lemonade concentrate
¾ cup simple syrup

Combine ingredients and stir until well blended.
Pour over ice. Garnish with lemon or orange slices.

Makes 8 to 10 servings.

SIMPLE SYRUP:

Simmer together ¾ cup water and ¾ cup sugar for 3 to 5 minutes.

PINK TEA

1 quart tea, cooled
2 cups cranberry juice cocktail

Juice of 1 lemon
2 tablespoons sugar

Combine ingredients. Serve over ice in tall glasses.

Makes 4 to 6 servings.

MINTED TEA

2 sprigs fresh mint
⅓ cup fresh or unsweet-ened orange juice
Juice of 2 lemons
2 cups strong hot tea

⅓ teaspoon powdered ginger
⅓ cup hot water
1 cup cold water

Bruise mint leaves in bowl or pitcher.

Pour in fruit juices and hot tea.

Stir ginger into the hot water, then blend with cold water. Add this to the fruit-juice-tea mixture.

Chill for 1 hour or more.

Makes 4 to 5 servings.

TEA PLANTER'S PUNCH

⅓ cup grenadine syrup
1 teaspoon almond
  flavoring

1 can (6 ounces) frozen
  lemonade concentrate
2 quarts strong tea, cooled

Stir grenadine syrup, almond flavoring, and lemonade concentrate into the cooled tea.

Serve in tall glasses with ice. Garnish with pineapple wedge, lemon slice, and cherry.

Makes 8 servings.

PLANTATION PUNCH

1 can (6 ounces) frozen
  orange juice
1 can (6 ounces) frozen
  grape juice

1 can (6 ounces) frozen
  lemonade concentrate
2 quarts strong tea,
  cooled
1 quart ginger ale

Stir frozen fruit juices and lemonade into cooled tea. Pour over a block of ice in a punch bowl.

Just before serving, add ginger ale. Garnish with thin slices of orange and lemon. *Makes 30 punch-cup servings.*

ROMAN PUNCH

1 cup sugar
2 cups boiling water
2 cups strong tea,
   cooled

1 cup orange juice
⅓ cup lemon juice
1 tablespoon rum extract
1 quart ginger ale

Stir sugar into boiling water. When sugar is dissolved, add remaining ingredients and serve over ice.

Makes 8 to 10 large servings.

HOSPITALITY TEA PUNCH

2 quarts boiling water
15 tea bags
2 cups lemon juice
1 quart orange juice

1½ quarts grape juice
2 cups sugar
2 quarts cold water
1 quart ginger ale

Pour boiling water over tea bags. Steep 3 to 5 minutes and remove tea bags. Cool tea.

Stir in all remaining ingredients except ginger ale.

Add ginger ale and ice cubes just before serving.

Makes 2 gallons of punch.

MINT TEA PUNCH

1 cup mint syrup
1 can (6 ounces) frozen lemonade concentrate
2¼ quarts strong tea, cooled

Stir mint syrup and frozen lemonade concentrate into tea. Pour over ice and serve in a punch bowl.

Garnish with slices of orange and lemon.

Makes 10 to 12 servings.

MINT SYRUP:

> 20 to 30 fresh mint leaves or 1 tablespoon mint jelly
> 1 cup sugar
> 1 cup water

Bruise mint leaves in sugar. Add water and stir over heat until sugar dissolves. Simmer 3 to 5 minutes.

Strain out leaves. If fresh mint is not available, combine sugar, water, and mint jelly. Heat and stir until dissolved.

STRAWBERRY TEA PUNCH

> 2 quarts strong tea, cooled
> 1 can (6 ounces) frozen lemonade concentrate
> ½ cup sugar
> 1 package (10 ounces) frozen strawberries

Stir sugar, lemonade concentrate, and frozen strawberries into cooled tea.

Serve over ice in punch cups or glasses.

Makes 8 to 10 servings.

PINEAPPLE PUNCH

Measure into each glass:

2 tablespoons pineapple
  juice
1 tablespoon lemon juice

2 to 3 teaspoons sugar
¾ cup tea
Ice cubes

Stir well with iced teaspoon. Garnish with thin slices of lemon and sprig of mint.

RHUBARB PUNCH

1 quart tea
1 quart rhubarb, cut into
  ½-inch pieces

1 lemon, cut into sections
1½ cups sugar

Combine tea, rhubarb, lemon, and sugar. Cook until rhubarb is tender. Strain and cool.

Serve punch in glasses over ice cubes.

Makes 4 to 6 servings.

CRANBERRY TEA PUNCH

2½ cups boiling water
5 tea bags
¼ teaspoon ground
  cinnamon
¼ teaspoon ground nut-
  meg

¾ cup sugar
1 pint cranberry juice
  cocktail
1½ cups water
½ cup orange juice
⅓ cup lemon juice

Pour boiling water over tea and spices. Cover and let steep 5 minutes.

Stir in sugar, then cool. Add remaining ingredients and chill. Serve garnished with lemon slices.

Makes 6 to 8 servings.

HOT SPICED AFTERNOON TEA

1 teaspoon whole cloves
1 cinnamon stick (2
    inches long)
4 quarts boiling water

15 tea bags
1¼ cups sugar
1 cup orange juice
¾ cup lemon juice

Add spices to water and bring to full rolling boil. Remove from heat and immediately add tea bags.

Steep for 4 minutes. Strain.

Add sugar and stir until dissolved. Pour in fruit juices.

Keep spiced tea hot or reheat over low heat, but do not boil. *Makes about 30 punch cups of tea.*

HOT TEA PUNCH

1 can (6 ounces) frozen
    lemonade concentrate
2 cinnamon sticks
    (2 inches long)

¼ cup honey
½ cup sugar
2 quarts strong tea

Stir ingredients into tea and simmer 10 minutes.

Serve in mugs or teacups.

Makes 10 to 12 servings.

"BRISK" TEA PUNCH

6 quarts boiling water
18 tea bags
3 tablespoons whole
 cloves

12 cinnamon sticks
 (2 inches long)
3 cups orange juice
¾ cup lemon juice
2 cups honey

Pour boiling water over tea bags and spices; let steep 3 to 5 minutes. Strain.

Add fruit juices and honey. Stir until well blended.

Serve hot in mugs garnished with orange slices.

Makes 24 servings.

HOT FRUIT PUNCH

1 cup strong tea
1 cup pineapple juice
1 cup orange juice
2 cups water

¼ cup sugar
6 pineapple spears
24 whole cloves

Combine tea, fruit juices, water, and sugar.

Heat to a boil.

Place clove-studded pineapple spear in each mug and pour in hot punch.

Makes 4 to 6 servings.

NEW ENGLAND SPECIAL

1 orange
12 whole cloves
1 cinnamon stick (2
    inches long) broken
    into pieces
4 tea bags

4 cups boiling water
1 cup cranberry juice
⅓ to ½ cup sugar
1½ to 2 teaspoons rum
    flavoring

Stud orange with cloves and cut into 6 or 8 sections. Drop sections into teapot, squeezing each section slightly. Add cinnamon, tea, and boiling water. Steep for 5 minutes and strain.

Stir in cranberry juice, sugar, and rum flavoring.

Makes 4 to 6 servings.

SKI TEA

4 lemon slices
8 whole cloves
4 cinnamon sticks
    (2 inches long)

4 tablespoons honey
1 quart hot tea

Stud each lemon slice with two cloves and place with a stick of cinnamon in each mug.

Stir honey into hot tea and pour into mugs.

Makes 4 servings.

HOT TOMATO-TEA COCKTAIL

2 cups tea
2 cups tomato juice
   cocktail

1 teaspoon salt
1 teaspoon Worcester-
   shire sauce

Combine all ingredients and heat to boiling.
   Serve in cups or mugs for first course of dinner.

Makes 6 servings.

CAMPAIGN TEA PUNCH

½ cup instant tea
2 quarts water
1 can (6 ounces) frozen
   limeade concentrate
1 can (6 ounces) frozen
   lemonade concentrate

1 can (6 ounces) frozen
   pineapple juice con-
   centrate
1 pint cranberry juice
   cocktail
1 bottle (1 pint) cold
   ginger ale

In large container, place instant tea. Gradually add water, stirring, until tea is thoroughly dissolved.

Then add limeade, lemonade, and pineapple juice concentrates and cranberry juice cocktail. Stir to blend well.

Just before serving, pour into punch bowl, add ginger ale and ice cubes.

Makes about 1 gallon or 25 5-ounce servings.

HOT TEA PUNCH

2 quarts tea
1 can (6 ounces) frozen
   lemonade concentrate,
   thawed

¼ cup honey
½ cup granulated sugar
2 cinnamon sticks
   (2 inches long)

In a 3-quart saucepan, combine tea with lemonade concentrate, honey, and sugar. Add cinnamon sticks and simmer 10 minutes.

Serve in mugs or teacups.

Makes about 14 5-ounce servings.

TEA CIDER PUNCH

½ cup instant tea
1 quart water
2 quarts apple cider
8 whole cloves

1 cinnamon stick
   (2 inches long)
2 tablespoons red cinnamon candy drops
½ cup granulated sugar
Juice of 1 lemon

In a 4-quart saucepan, stir instant tea into water and cider; add cloves, cinnamon stick, candy drops, sugar, and lemon juice. Beat, stirring occasionally but do not boil.

Ladle into cups.

Makes 3 quarts, or about 18 5-ounce servings.

TEA RITUALS AND CUSTOMS AROUND THE WORLD

History indicates that the ancient Chinese learned of tea drinking from the aboriginal tribesmen of southwestern China. The beverage was made by boiling the raw green leaves of wild tea plants in kettles over smoky outdoor fires. This early tea drinking was the beginning of what later developed into Chinese and Japanese socioreligious rites of infinite refinement.

Throughout the early centuries tea was *always* taken as a remedy for human ailments. By 780 A.D. the Chinese tea code was so rigid in its requirements that no fashionable family was without the prescribed implements for serving tea. The cabinets in which these ceremonial instruments were stored were fashioned with patient artistry by the finest craftsmen of the day. The quality of the decorative detail marked the social standing of the family. Only the master of the house was permitted to handle the precious tea tools and preside over the serving of tea.

The oldest Chinese method of tea making was to boil powdered tea with rice cakes until a thick syrup formed to which ginger was added. At first the Chinese didn't necessarily use a teapot, and tea leaves were usually placed in a cup with a cover but no handles. The cup was filled with hot but not boiling water, and the cover—which resembled an overturned saucer—was placed on top of the cup. When the drinker raised the cup to his lips, he lifted the cover slightly with his forefinger, just enough to drain the liquid to be strained into his mouth. Tea was taken in this manner on all occasions and it was always offered to guests. In the cities of China *kwans* or teahouses were numerous, and, similar to the cafés of other countries, they enjoyed a flourishing business and had a regular clientele which gathered daily at certain hours. The habitués of the *kwans* brought along their own tea leaves, and after paying a small fixed sum they were free to sit at the tables as long as they wished and were served as much hot water as they desired.

Tea drinking reached its supreme importance, however, in Japan. There, the rites of the tea ceremony were observed according to the strict code set down by the first great tea master, Shuko, and carried out under the patronage of shogun Yoshimasa (1443–73), who built in Kyoto a beautiful silver pavilion which housed the first tearoom. First used as a medicinal potion, tea was regarded as a sacred remedy upon which the cult of "teaism," the worship of the beautiful and harmonious in nature and life, was predicated. Tea drinking with meditation became a temple ritual and later developed into the most popular adjunct to social intercourse. In fact, tea was the *only* beverage which was considered to be socially correct.

Any discussion of the customs of tea drinking must start with a description of the Japanese tea ceremony itself.

We know that according to legend tea was said to have grown from the fallen eyelids of Daruma. But aside from the legend, historians state that in the period of 794–1159 A.D. the Buddhist culture in Japan made tea drinking a pretext for religious and poetic conversation. With these events, a regular ceremony evolved. Gradually tea drinking extended from the religious orders to the laity, who fixed upon the custom as an occasion for learned discourse of a religious nature and not infrequently of political purpose as well.

The esthetic rite which was practiced at these discourses was known as *Cha-no-yu*, which means "hot water tea." At first the meetings were held in the temple groves where all was harmonious with the solemn gathering. In towns, these conditions were simulated in little rooms which were set apart in the garden. No frivolous conversation was sanctioned in the tearoom. Only the most simple movements were performed in accordance with the strictest formalities of the ceremony, and only prescribed behavior patterns were acceptable.

The philosophy behind teaism is the basis for a cult founded on the worship of the beautiful and the love of nature. Simplicity of materials is the keynote. Teaism inculcates purity, harmony, and mutual forbearance. It has been a dominant force in the shaping of the manners and customs of the Japanese. Its influence can be seen in their porcelain, lacquer, painting, and literature. The central theme of teaism is the concept that greatness is inherent in the smallest incidents of life. It teaches that art does not exist only for the wealthy but that it is to be found in the most unpretentious endeavors of the humble.

The tea ceremony is performed in a tearoom which accommodates exactly four and a half mats. Guests wash their hands and faces and remove their sandals before entering the tearoom through a panel two feet square. This doorway is purposely made low to bring the tea drinker immediately to the physical position which connotes humility. Inside the *cha-shitsu* the guests admire the decorations and flower arrangement while the host collects his implements. Frequently the beauty of the utensils causes admiration. During the ceremony the guests sit cross-legged on mats. The host places a spoonful of powdered tea in a special tea bowl. A dipperful of boiling water is taken from a kettle simmering on a charcoal firebox and placed over the tea. The mixture is stirred with a small bamboo whisk resembling an old-fashioned shaving brush, and each movement made by the host has symbolic significance. When the tea is ready, the tea drinker receives the dish of tea or *cha-wan* with a specially folded napkin. The bowl is held in the palm of the left hand, supported by the thumb and fingers of the right hand. It is raised to the forehead and lowered with a slight turn to the right. A drink is taken, and the bowl is returned to its original position. During the last movement the bowl is given a half turn to the right, placing the side which has been touched by the lips of the drinker in the opposite position. The cup is wiped with the napkin before it is passed to the next person.

As the tea ceremony developed it became the practice to serve individual tea bowls from which guests sip the tea slowly, leaving a few drops of tea in each bowl. At the end of the tea drinking the guest must throw back his head and drink this final draught with a distinct sucking sound to show his host his complete satisfaction with the beverage. The host apologizes for the poor quality of the tea, as an act of politeness, and the entire group admires the empty serving bowl, which is often an antique of rare beauty and important historical significance. The ceremony is ended.

After the cups and tea implements are washed, the guests depart with many farewell bows to the host, who kneels at the door through which they pass.

At least three years of instruction and practice are considered necessary for achieving proficiency in the serving of the ceremonial tea. But this formal technique has nothing to do with the ordinary tea drinking of the people of Japan, who prepare their tea just as we do. Green teas are favored, and they are served without sugar or milk in small cups without handles. Teahouses are found everywhere, and at railway stations tea is sold to travelers. Everywhere at every time of the day Japanese enjoy tea.

Koreans find the same enjoyment in Japanese teas, which they brew by throwing the tea leaves into a kettle of boiling water. Many Koreans like the taste of a raw egg between sips of tea, and rice cakes are frequently eaten at teatime.

In Burma, tea leaves are prepared as a salad called *letpet*.

Letpet is a kind of pickled tea made by soaking tea leaves in oil and garlic. Sometimes dried fish is eaten with the dish.

Tea leaves have a ceremonial significance in Burma and are thought to ensure the conjugal bliss of newlyweds who drink from the same cup a mixture of tea leaves which have been steeped in oil.

Thailand's people like a special tea they call *miang*. The tea leaves are seasoned with salt and other condiments and then they are chewed.

Almost every tea drinker is familiar with two of the world's finest teas: those from Assam and those from Darjeeling, both in India, the fascinating land of many faces.

Before the British came to India, her people did not take tea. Tea is alien to Hindu culture and therefore has no religious significance as it has in China and Japan. Today, of course, tea drinking has become absorbed into every facet of the life of India.

Living in one of the world's largest tea-producing countries, the Indian people have become accustomed to drinking tea upon arising, at breakfast, at four in the afternoon, and before bedtime. At one time Indian ladies gathered together for a midmorning teatime called "elevenses," but this custom, which is tantamount to the American coffee klatch, has gradually fallen into disuse.

In the cities, Indians brew tea just as it is done in England and America. It is served plain or with sugar and milk. Cream is never used, as it is thought to "coat" the tea flavor. But in rural India, tea is still brewed according to older custom. Water is set to boil, over an open fire, in a flat pan called a *dekchi*. Tea leaves are added to the boiling water and a tight lid is fitted onto the *dekchi*. When the brew is ready it is ladled out and drunk from mugs or unglazed clay bowls called *khulahs*.

Tea is the national beverage of Ceylon, another of the largest of the world's tea producers. The Ceylonese are followers of the English tea customs. Hot tea is served upon arising, again at breakfast, in midmorning and midafternoon, and as a night cap. In native custom it may be served from the finest tea service in the house to guests who sit comfortably among pillows spread on the floor, but for the most part the Ceylonese drink tea at tea tables in the style of the West.

Out in the countryside of Ceylon, tea boutiques, each identified by a cluster of bananas hanging in front of the entry, are numerous. Villagers frequently stop off at them on their way home from work in the fruitful tea gardens which cover the slopes of the country. The water for the tea is brewed in an urn which resembles a samovar. The tea is placed in a cloth strainer through which the boiling water is poured. The water trickles through the leaves into a brass cup and is poured from one brass cup to another until it is sufficiently cool to drink. In Ceylon, tea is taken without milk, but sugar or "jaggery," sugar from the palm, is sometimes used.

Beautiful hand-carved silver tea sets are featured at the tea tables of Indonesia, where tea is brewed right in the teapot. The pot is filled with water, and the tea leaves are added and release their flavor while the kettle is still being heated.

In the past, the Indonesian national custom was to enjoy tea with guests seated on pillows on the floor around a low serving table or mat. But most of today's Indonesians, though they brew their tea differently from the way we do, take their tea around the traditional type of tea table in much the same manner as do the people of India and Ceylon.

Iranians drink tea twenty-four hours a day. At breakfast, tea is taken with the meal itself, but at other meals tea is enjoyed only after dessert. Iranians even offer tea to their evening guests. Perfumed tea is a great favorite, and often scented flowers or herbs are kept with tea leaves in closed containers for several days before the leaves are used.

Traditionally the oldest woman of the Iranian family presides over the tea serving, sitting on a rug especially reserved for the tea ceremony. The tea essence is poured into a small glass which is placed in a silver holder. Hot water is added from a samovar according to the strength desired. Sugar and lemon are always served with tea in Iran even though the tea is perfumed.

Lying in the ocean below the countries of tea-drinking Asia is the land known as "Down Under." Peopled by hearty, spirited men and women who adhere to British tea customs, the land of Australia is full of persons who drink tea seven times a day—before breakfast, with breakfast, at eleven in the morning, at four in the afternoon, at dinner, and before bedtime. The tea is made and served in the traditional British manner.

On the broad prairies, however, tea drinking is quite a different matter. At all times the rugged Australian sheep raisers, who rank as the tallest of civilized men, carry with them a smoke-blackened tin called a "billycan" in which they make their tea. The "Sundowners," as these rugged outdoorsmen are called, rise in the morning, heat water to boil in the billycan, and throw in a handful of tea leaves. While they prepare the rest of the breakfast they leave the tea to cook until it is well stewed. The billycan remains on the fire all day while the Sundowner is at work, and in the evening when he returns he rekindles the fire under the billycan and reheats the black decoction it contains, adds plenty of sugar and perhaps a gumtree leaf for flavor, and downs the beverage with gusto. When the Bushman is on the move, his billycan is carried in his bedroll or "swag," which has been curiously called "Matilda" and has become world-famous through the words and music of the rollicking tune "Waltzing Matilda."

New Zealanders find tea so important that they too drink it seven times a day just like the Aussies.

Crossing over to the African continent, we find tea taken in many countries. In South Africa, British tea habits prevail, while in Egypt tea is prepared in the British manner but served in glasses and flavored with sugar only. Algerians have always preferred green teas but like a touch of mint to heighten the taste. The people of Morocco adore tea, and as a beverage of social intercourse it holds an important position in their way of life. In many wealthy Moorish homes a tea maker is retained as a specialist among the servants, but in most residences the tea is prepared by the host. The tea leaves are placed in a brass or silver teapot to which sugar and mint are added. Boiling water is poured over them, and the host repeatedly tastes the tea while it is brewing until he is certain that the flavor will satisfy the guests. The tea is served in small glasses decorated with sprigs of mint. Guests never put sugar in their glasses because the host has already flavored the tea. Protocol says that if the guest accepts the offer of tea, he must drink at least three glasses of it. Favorite teatime delicacies which accompany Moorish tea are almond crescents and stuffed walnuts called *tmarh*.

We have read that the first European tea drinkers were the Jesuit priests serving in China and Japan during the sixteenth century, and we know that the accounts they wrote home encouraged Dutch traders to follow the Portuguese in their venturesome forays to the Orient. By early in the seventeenth century the patrons of the Dutch East India Company were introducing tea drinking at their receptions and treating tea as an expensive and exotic novelty. At first tea was used only at the entertainments of the rich and famous, but by 1660 every housewife in the Netherlands had a tearoom in her home. The popularity of tea drinking crossed the English Channel, and served at the court of England and at the meetings of the English East India Company, tea was coveted as a luxury.

When tea drinking was first introduced by the great tea companies of England there was actually public resistance to it. The populace suspected the ulterior motives of the East India Company. Englishmen enjoyed their repose in the coffeehouses to which they had become accustomed and were quite content with the status quo. After 1660, when Thomas Garway started to serve tea as well as coffee in his coffeehouse, tea drinking became *à la mode*.

To be sure, the new vogue came under attack from fanatics

who considered it an evil in which men took time from productive work. But tea drinking was staunchly defended by those who loved it, most notably the redoubtable Dr. Johnson, formidable lexicographer, who was said to be able to drink as many as twelve cups of tea at one sitting. Other famous Englishmen who defended tea were Gladstone, the great Parliamentarian, the poet Coleridge, and the essayist De Quincey, all of whom consumed prodigious amounts of the refreshing amber liquid each day.

In the early eighteenth century outdoor tea gardens were considered ideal for relaxation, entertainment, and games. Sporting fields abounded, variety programs and concerts were given, and dancing, gambling, and racing were all encouraged. At first there was no admission charge for these pleasures. Cheeses, cake, coffee, and tea as well as ale could be purchased. Later, however, a fixed admission was charged in addition to the price of the refreshments. Sparkling lanterns, lit by candles, adorned the pleasure grounds. People, handsomely dressed, promenaded on flowered paths under spreading trees. Now these gay gardens of yesterday are gone and most of the time Britishers take their tea indoors. Black teas of India and Ceylon are used, and tea is made by placing a teaspoonful of tea for each cup, plus one for the pot, into a teapot which has been previously warmed. The tea is infused for about five minutes with fresh boiling water, and frequently the liquor will be poured into another warmed teapot to avoid astringency. Milk and cream are generally placed in the cup *before* the tea is poured. In restaurants extra hot water is served so that two or three cups can be made.

Britishers take tea for breakfast and lunch. Afternoon tea in the United Kingdom is considered a most charming time of reunion—a prelude to late dining when tea is again served.

So important is afternoon tea in England that motorized teashops make stops along the roads to serve tea to motorists. Chains of tearooms serve tea throughout day and evening. Some special tearooms supply music for tea dancing, and in

85

warm weather Britishers like to take their afternoon tea in the open air in surroundings that are restful. Tea gardens are operated in London in public parks such as Hyde Park, Kensington Gardens, and Kew Gardens, and in the suburbs tea is served in a number of private houses where little signs are displayed upon which one reads the word *TEAS*. The lounges of many English hotels offer tea, as do large theaters and cinemas. Tea is important at all social affairs and can be purchased at regattas, cricket matches, the Ascot races, and the like. It is served on all British railways and on all British-owned ocean liners and airplanes. Four o'clock tea is, of course, served to businessmen in their offices.

For those Englishmen who take their principle meal at midday "high tea" is customary. Served at six o'clock, it is a quite substantial tea, and includes meat. Generally it replaces the evening meal.

No matter what the time of day, what the weather, the loyal Briton wants to have a *good* cup of tea whenever he is in the mood.

Canadians feel much the same way about good tea.

The first shipment of tea sent to Canada was slated to reach Hudson Bay in 1715, but bad sailing weather kept the boatload of precious leaf from reaching Canadian shores before 1716. Welcomed with enthusiasm, tea was later carried out to the broad plains of the Canadian West in the covered wagons and oxcarts of the pioneers.

Today Canadians consume over eleven billion cups of tea a year, made principally from the black teas. They are very particular as to how it is made, and insist that the crockery teapot be thoroughly heated before the leaves are placed in it. Canadians prefer sugar and cream in their tea to taking it plain or with lemon. Tea is served at breakfast, before retiring, and with other meals and snacks throughout the day. Tea bags are frequently used and instant tea is gaining in popularity. Canadians are the only ones who join Americans in their love of iced tea. Five o'clock tea is served in modern hotels just as it is in England, and most of the department stores have tearooms where foot-weary shoppers can "pep up" with tea.

The neighbors of Canada who inhabit New Brunswick, Nova Scotia, and Newfoundland prepare their tea much as it is prepared in the United Kingdom. But, like most tea drinkers of the Western Hemisphere, they use tea bags and instant tea as well as tea leaves in brewing their favorite beverage.

In order to understand more fully the manners and customs of American tea drinking it is necessary to return our attention to the habits of Europe during the seventeenth century.

While the Portuguese and Dutch were bringing spices and tea to Western Europe tea was also being transported by camel caravan from China, across mountains and deserts to Eastern Europe. In 1618 the journey took eighteen months. The Russians failed to show much enthusiasm for tea at the time, although a report from a young German in residence at the German Embassy in Moscow in the years 1633–34 states that tea was served at the official breakfast meetings of diplomats.

Even though the Russians, like the English, were slow in accepting tea, in the past three centuries they have become tea connoisseurs.

Russian tea is made in a rather unique fashion. Water is heated in a samovar—a large, graceful metal boiler made hot by placing charcoal in the metal pipe which runs through its center. The teapot containing the tea essence rests on the saucer-shaped top of the samovar. When serving the tea the hostess uses tall glasses encased in metal holders which are similar to those we use at American soda fountains. She pours each glass one quarter full of tea essence and then fills the glass with boiling water from the samovar. For flavoring she offers her guests lemon but no milk or cream. Russians prefer to flavor their tea with jam, or they may place a lump of sugar on their tongue and sip the tea through the sugar.

In cold weather, liquor is sometimes added to fortify the tea drinker against the outdoor climate. In some districts of Russia cups and mugs are favored over glasses.

Farther to the north in the coldest corner of Europe, Laplanders brew tea in a large bowl which is passed from hand to hand by the members of the family.

With Russia, England, and the Netherlands as exceptions, it is interesting to observe that the inhabitants of other European countries are not tea drinkers to any great extent. As a rule, Austrians, Hungarians, and Czechs who *do* drink tea mix it with rum, lemon, or milk. Greeks prefer to drink it an hour or so after dinner as a digestive, and Poles like their tea *à la russe*. Tea drinking in France is confined to those citizens who particularly esteem the beverage. Most of these tea drinkers are members of the large colonies of English, Americans, and Russians who have taken up residence in this country of marvelous wines and strong, fragrant demitasse coffee. In fairness to their culinary creativity, however, it is important to credit the French with the innovation of adding cream and milk to tea. It is a contribution to tea drinking for which many imbibers are exceedingly grateful and illustrates to a great degree the gift which the French have for gastronomic discovery.

Afternoon tea has become a popular means of passing a social hour in the more cosmopolitan of Italian cities. The tea is served with sugar, milk, or lemon, and flaky Florentine and Neapolitan pastries enhance the afternoon "tea break."

The leading tea drinkers of Europe are the people of the Netherlands. They favor the fermented teas of Java, India, and Ceylon. A Netherlands hostess prepares her tea by infusing it with freshly boiled water for no longer than five to six minutes. The teapot is placed under a tea cozy to retain warmth. Tea is enjoyed at breakfast and in the afternoon, and it is offered to all visitors who drop by. Netherlanders also value a cup of tea an hour after dinner as an aid to digestion since their meals are plentiful.

When the Dutch housewives crossed the ocean to New Amsterdam they brought with them to the New World their custom of afternoon tea. They carried along their teaboards, teapots, "bite and stir" boxes partitioned in two parts to hold lumps of sugar and powdered sugar, silver spoons, strainers, and other aids to proper tea making and tea serving. The socially correct New Amsterdam hostess brewed several kinds of tea simultaneously to cater to the tastes of her guests, and with the tea she offered sugar and saffron or peach leaves for flavoring. Hot muffins, waffles, and wafers were served, and an *ooma*, or sifter, containing a mixture of sugar and cinnamon was always present on the table. When New Amsterdam became New York, English tea customs were adopted. Tea gardens were opened for breakfast as well as for evening entertainment. Some of them were located at the site of natural springs "out of town" (what is now Park Row in the Wall Street area). Only the freshest water was provided from these springs for the making of tea. Special pumps were attached to three other springs in the "uptown" area, and in 1757 it was thought necessary to pass a law for the "Regulation of the Tea Water Men in the City of New York" to make certain that the supply was not exceeded by the demand.

By the beginning of the eighteenth century tea drinking had an influence on furnishings, china, and silverware. Objects of great cost and beauty were created by the greatest artisans of the period. Stoneware, faïence, earthenware, the cream-colored ware of Staffordshire, and the Queensware and Jasperware of Wedgwood were all fashioned into tea sets. The making of English porcelain teapots became a fine art, and the Liverpool Museum contains marvelous examples of tea porcelain of the period. Examples of the potter's art were carried by young English craftsmen to our shores, and American pottery making was begun.

The great period of art pottery passed with the general adoption of the art of transfer printing, and on both sides of the ocean hand-wrought teapots and tea implements were fashioned of silver, Sheffield plate, or pewter. Exquisite tea sets and tea accessories from this period of history show a general beauty of form and decoration. Tea caddies, tea-spoons, and other articles for tea serving continued to be made—the masterpieces moving in cycles from the simplicity of the seventeenth century to the ornate embellishments associated with the end of the nineteenth. Recent modern silver designs tend to return to the graceful, simple, curved lines and broad, plain surfaces of the silverware that was popular at the outset of American tea drinking. There has been a great upsurge in interest in early silversmiths like Paul Revere. Early tea sets can be seen in the Thomas J. Lipton Collection and in the Clearwater Collection of the Metropolitan Museum of Art, in New York City, which contains some magnificent examples of the American teapot maker's art.

It was with the deepest regret that the patriotic colonial hostesses abandoned their handsome tea tables, their gleaming tea sets, and their varied-colored tea plates, cups, and saucers during the tea boycott which led to the famous events of the Revolution, but we have seen how, in the era of the great clipper ships, American interest in tea was restored.

During the century which followed, American liberty and American enterprise attracted men and women from all the countries of the world. In every case they brought with them the tea manners and customs of their countries of origin. America became once more a nation of tea drinkers.

Although Americans preferred to drink green tea before World War I, our tastes have changed gradually until over 90 per cent of the tea we drink now is black tea. Our tea-drinking habits, because we are a melting-pot culture, vary a great deal: 30 per cent of our citizens take milk and sugar with their tea, almost 27 per cent use only sugar, 16 per cent sugar and lemon, 14 per cent drink it plain; and those falling into the other percentages use just milk, just lemon, or some individually contrived combination of these flavorings.

Our greatest peculiarity as tea consumers is our universally wide use of tea bags. These were invented in 1908 as an advertising idea by a promotion-minded wholesaler named Thomas Sullivan, who sent his customers tea samples tied in little bags of China silk. The customers, finding tea in this form exceedingly convenient, demanded more and more of these little packets. Modern tea bags, conserving the principle set up by Mr. Sullivan, have been adapted to the use of the most efficient filter papers filled with exactly one teaspoon of tea, just the right amount for the perfect cup of the beverage.

A purely American twist on tea drinking is our national enthusiasm for iced tea. Introduced to Americans in 1904 at the Louisiana Purchase Exposition in St. Louis, Missouri, it has become America's favorite summer beverage. It is savored for its stimulating and bracing effect and makes up a great part of the phenomenal number of cups of tea which we drink annually whether at mealtime, as an afternoon distraction from our work routine, or as a pleasant soothing beverage during the evening, or before bed.

The ancient *ch'a* of China has reached its ultimate goal. It has encircled the globe and has become an integral part of American mealtime, and social festivity.

"TEA AND..." FAVORITES FROM AROUND THE WORLD

AUSTRALIAN TRIFLE

1 package bakery
  ladyfingers
Raspberry or apricot
  jam or marmalade
¼ cup sherry or brandy

1 package instant
  vanilla pudding mix
½ cup heavy cream,
  whipped

Split ladyfingers. Spread ladyfingers generously with jam. Stand them up along the sides of a large dessert dish, or individual dishes. Sprinkle with sherry or brandy and let stand until cake is moistened.

Make instant pudding according to directions on package for custard sauce. When thickened, stir to smoothness, and pour into cake-lined dish or dishes to cover no more than ¾ of the cake. Chill.

When ready to serve, top with whipped cream. Garnish with dash of jam.

Makes 6 servings.

DAMPER

(AUSTRALIA)

> 2 cups biscuit mix
> ⅔ cup milk

Measure biscuit mix into bowl, add milk all at once, and stir with fork to blend. Turn out on floured board and knead about 10 times. Put on ungreased cookie sheet, and press into a circle (about 8 inches in diameter). Cut partway through into 6 or 8 wedges.

Bake in a 450° F. oven 15 to 20 minutes, until lightly browned and firm in the center.

Cut into previously scored wedges, and serve warm.

If your taste for teatime accompaniments runs to the sweet side, a topping of brown sugar crumbled with butter may be added before baking.

Makes 6 to 8 servings.

CURRY-CHEESE BISCUITS

(AUSTRALIA)

> 2 cups sifted all-purpose flour
> ½ teaspoon salt
> ½ teaspoon powdered dry mustard
> 1½ teaspoons curry powder
> 1/16 teaspoon ground cayenne pepper
> ⅔ cup butter or margarine
> 1 cup grated sharp cheddar cheese
> 1 egg, beaten
> 2 tablespoons milk

Combine the first five ingredients in a mixing bowl. Add butter or margarine and cut it in to fine crumb consistency. Blend in cheese. Stir in beaten egg and milk.

Turn out onto a pastry board while still in the crumbly stage. Form into a mound with hands. Cut through the center of mound with a spatula. Stack half of the crumbly mound on the other half and again shape into a mound. Repeat this process until the dough holds together, about 10 to 12 times.

Roll into 1/16-inch thickness. Cut with a 2-inch cookie cutter. Bake in a 400° F. oven 10 minutes.

Makes 66 biscuits.

DEVONSHIRE SCONES

(ENGLAND)

2 cups sifted all-purpose flour	½ teaspoon salt
2 tablespoons sugar	⅓ cup butter or margarine
2½ teaspoons baking powder	2 eggs
	5 tablespoons milk

Sift together flour, sugar, baking powder, and salt into a bowl. Cut in margarine until mixture resembles coarse cornmeal.

Add eggs to milk and blend well; stir into flour mixture.

Turn out on lightly floured surface. Knead lightly; roll out or pat to ½-inch thickness. Cut into small triangles. Place on floured baking sheet. Brush with milk and sprinkle lightly with sugar, if desired.

Bake in a 450° F. oven 8 to 10 minutes, or until golden. Cool on wire rack.

Serve warm with accompanying small bowls of whipped cream cheese and strawberry preserves so that guests can split their own and spread first with cheese, then preserves.

Makes 2 dozen scones.

HALWA

(INDIA)

2 cups water
1 cup sugar
1 cup (2 sticks) butter or
  margarine
1½ cups farina
⅔ cup seeded raisins
¼ cup flaked coconut

⅔ cup coarsely chopped
  blanched almonds
½ teaspoon ground
  cardamom
1 teaspoon ground
  cinnamon

Combine water and sugar in saucepan. Boil about 10 minutes, or until a thin syrup forms.

Melt butter in another pan, add farina, and cook and stir over low heat until very lightly browned.

Add raisins, coconut, almonds, spices, and hot sugar syrup. Blend thoroughly.

While still warm, press into a greased 8x8x2-inch pan in an even layer. Cool at room temperature until set. Cut in 2-inch squares and chill.

Makes 16 squares.

PILUS (SWEET POTATO BALLS)

(INDONESIA)

2 cups cooked mashed
  sweet potatoes
1 tablespoon flour
1½ tablespoons sugar

1 egg
Vegetable oil
Confectioners' sugar

Mix potatoes, flour, sugar, and egg thoroughly. Form small balls (1-inch diameter). Deep fry and drain.

Sprinkle with confectioners' sugar.

PISANG GORENG (BANANA FRITTERS)

(INDONESIA)

4 *mashed ripe bananas*	3 *tablespoons sugar*
¾ *cup flour*	*Vegetable oil*
2 *eggs, beaten*	*Cinnamon sugar*

Combine all ingredients. Mix thoroughly and beat slightly.

Take 1 full tablespoon of this mixture for each cake. Fry on both sides.

Serve with cinnamon sugar.

NANE SHIRINI

(IRAN)

2 *cups flour*	1 *teaspoon pure vanilla extract*
1 *teaspoon baking powder*	
1 *cup vegetable shortening*	1 *teaspoon almond extract*
1 *cup granulated sugar*	1 *teaspoon lemon extract*
2 *egg yolks*	

Sift flour and baking powder together. Cream shortening and granulated sugar thoroughly. Blend in egg yolks, vanilla, almond, and lemon extracts. Mix well.

Gradually add the dry ingredients and mix until dough is well blended.

Roll dough into round balls with hands, using about 1 level teaspoon of dough for each ball. Place on ungreased baking sheet and flatten slightly with a spoon. Prick some of the cookies with the tines of a fork to give a little variety in appearance, if desired.

Bake in a 300° F. oven for 20 minutes.

Makes 30 to 40 cookies.

HOLLYT

(IRAQ)

1 *cup soft butter or mar-garine*

3 *cups sifted all-purpose flour*

1 *cup granulated sugar*

½ *teaspoon pure vanilla extract*

1 *cup finely chopped blanched almonds*

3 *tablespoons sugar*

½ *teaspoon pure vanilla extract*

In large electric mixer bowl, with mixer at "cream" or medium speed (or with spoon), mix butter with flour until thoroughly blended. Add 1 cup sugar, ½ teaspoon vanilla, and continue beating—about 4 minutes altogether. Refrigerate dough 15 minutes.

While dough is chilling, mix almonds, 3 tablespoons sugar, and ½ teaspoon vanilla for filling.

Divide dough in halves. Roll out half of dough between 2 sheets of waxed paper; cut into 24 2-inch squares.

Place 1 teaspoon nut mixture in center of each of 12 squares; top each one with one of remaining squares; seal all edges by pressing with tines of fork. Place on an ungreased cookie sheet. Bake in a 350° F. oven 15 to 20 minutes—they do not brown. Cool 10 minutes before removing from cookie sheet. Serve warm with favorite sauce.

Makes 24 cookies.

CREAM SCONES

(IRELAND)

2 cups sifted all-purpose flour

3 teaspoons baking powder

½ teaspoon salt

2 tablespoons granulated sugar

⅓ cup butter or margarine

2 eggs

½ cup (about) light cream or undiluted evaporated milk

Grease 2 cookie sheets.

Sift together into a bowl flour, baking powder, salt, and sugar. Add butter or margarine and cut it in finely with a pastry blender or 2 knives used scissors fashion.

Beat eggs well; stir in cream or evaporated milk.

Make a well in dry ingredients; add liquids and combine lightly, adding a little more milk, if necessary, to make a soft dough.

Turn out on floured board and knead lightly a dozen times. Divide dough into 2 equal portions and shape into smooth balls. Roll out one ball of dough into a round about ¾ inch thick. Place on the prepared cookie sheet. Cut the round of dough into 8 pie-shaped wedges, then draw them out so that the pieces are at least 1 inch apart. Repeat with other portion of dough. Bake in a 450° F. oven 8 to 10 minutes.

Meantime, if glaze is desired, combine 1 tablespoon cream or evaporated milk and 1 tablespoon granulated sugar. Immediately after scones are taken from the oven, brush tops with this mixture.

Makes 16 scones.

IRISH SODA BREAD

3 cups sifted enriched
  flour*
⅔ cup sugar
1 tablespoon baking
  powder
1 teaspoon soda
1 teaspoon salt

1½ cups currants or dark,
  seedless raisins
2 eggs, beaten
1¾ to 2 cups buttermilk
2 tablespoons melted
  butter or margarine

Sift together into a large bowl flour, sugar, baking powder, soda, and salt. Stir in currants or raisins. Combine eggs, buttermilk, and butter or margarine.

Add liquid mixture to dry ingredients and mix just until flour is moistened.

Turn batter into greased 5¼x9½-inch loaf pan. Bake in a 350° F. oven about 1 hour. Remove from pan immediately. Allow to cool thoroughly before slicing.

Makes 1 loaf.

* If self-rising flour is used, omit baking powder and salt

CHEESE TARTS

(IRELAND)

PASTRY:
  2 cups sifted all-purpose
    flour
  1 teaspoon salt
  ⅔ cup shortening
  4 to 5 tablespoons water
FILLING:
  2 eggs, unbeaten

2 tablespoons soft butter
  or margarine
1 cup granulated sugar
¼ cup undiluted evapo-
  rated milk
2 tablespoons lemon juice
½ cup chopped walnuts
2 cups seedless raisins

Pastry: Sift flour and salt into bowl. With pastry blender or 2 knives, scissors fashion, cut in shortening until it resembles coarse cornmeal. Sprinkle water, 1 tablespoon at a time, over the mixture; mix with fork. (Use only enough water to make flour particles cling together.)

Lightly form half of dough into smooth ball; roll out on floured surface. Cut into 10 3-inch squares. Repeat with rest of dough. Fit 20 2¾-inch muffin-pan cups with pastry squares, letting corners stand upright.

Filling: In large electric mixer bowl, with mixer at "cream" or medium speed, mix eggs, butter, and sugar until very light and fluffy—about 4 minutes altogether. At low speed or "blend," beat in milk, lemon juice, walnuts, and raisins. Fill unbaked tart shells ¾ full with mixture. Bake in a 350° F. oven 45 minutes or until firm. Cool 10 minutes before removing from muffin-pan cups.

Makes 20 tarts.

CHANUKAH BRAZIL NUT CAKE

(ISRAEL)

½ cup butter or vegetable shortening
1 cup sugar
⅓ cup orange juice
3 eggs
1 cup chopped Brazil nuts
¾ cup raisins
1 jar (8 ounces) mixed, diced candied fruits

2 cups sifted all-purpose flour, divided
¼ teaspoon salt
¼ teaspoon baking soda
2 teaspoons baking powder
1 teaspoon pure vanilla extract
¼ cup brandy (optional)

Cream butter or shortening; add sugar, and cream until light and fluffy. Blend in orange juice. Add eggs, one at a time, beating after each addition.

Mix together Brazil nuts, raisins, and candied fruits; stir in 1 cup of the flour.

Sift together remaining 1 cup flour with salt, soda, and baking powder.

Combine fruit-flour mixture and sifted dry ingredients with creamed mixture; mix well. Stir in vanilla and brandy.

Then turn into a waxed-paper-lined 9-inch tube pan. Bake in a 300° F. oven 1 hour, 50 minutes.

Makes 1 9-inch tube cake.

CHANUKAH SYMBOL COOKIES

(ISRAEL)

½ cup butter or
  margarine
1 cup sugar
1 egg
1 teaspoon grated orange
  rind
2 tablespoons orange
  juice

1 cup ground Brazil nuts
2 cups sifted all-purpose
  flour
2 teaspoons baking
  powder
½ teaspoon salt
¼ teaspoon almond
  flavoring

Cream butter; gradually add sugar and beat until light and fluffy. Stir in egg, orange rind, orange juice, and Brazil nuts.

Sift together flour, baking powder, and salt. Add to creamed mixture; mix well. Stir in almond flavoring. Chill several hours.

Roll out dough ⅛ inch thick on lightly floured board or pastry cloth. Cut into "dreidel" shape using a paper pattern, or cut into desired shapes with 2-inch cookie cutters. Bake on ungreased cookie sheets in a 375° F. oven 8 to 10 minutes.

Makes approximately 5 dozen cookies.

FALAFEL

(ISRAEL)

2 cups day-old bread
  cubes
¾ cup milk
1 can (1 pound) chick
  peas, drained
¼ teaspoon ground
  black pepper
Dash cayenne

¼ cup chopped parsley
1 tablespoon chopped dill
1 crushed clove garlic
½ teaspoon salt
2 tablespoons flour
2 tablespoons diced
  pimiento

In large bowl, soak bread cubes in milk.

Meanwhile, mash drained peas with fork; add black pepper, cayenne, parsley, dill, garlic, salt, flour, and pimiento.

Then squeeze milk from bread; add bread to pea mixture and mix well.

Into 2 inches deepfat, heated to 360° F., drop pea mixture by heaping tablespoons, a few at a time. Fry until golden brown, turning as needed. Serve hot as snack.

Makes about 16 falafel.

SIMITS

(TURKEY)

¾ cup warm (not hot)
  water
1 package active dry yeast

2½ cups biscuit mix
1 egg white

Sprinkle yeast over water and let dissolve. Add biscuit mix and beat to blend.

Turn out on floured board and knead about 20 times. Roll out into rectangle and cut into ½-inch strips. Cut strips into 3-inch lengths and roll with palms into tubular shape. Moisten ends of rolls and pinch together into circles.

Put on ungreased cookie sheet and brush with unbeaten egg white (sesame seeds may be sprinkled on top if desired). Bake in a 425° F. oven 15 to 20 minutes until lightly browned.

Serve either warm or cold, with good hot tea and cubes of cheese.

Makes about 20 simits.

KESTANE SEKERI (CHESTNUT SOUFFLE)

(TURKEY)

1 cup (½ pound) chest-nuts (or 9½-ounce jar marrons)	3 tablespoons sugar
	4 eggs, separated
	1 tablespoon brandy or sherry
⅛ teaspoon salt	
2 tablespoons butter	
2 tablespoons heavy cream	1 teaspoon pure vanilla extract

If fresh chestnuts are used, parboil and remove skins. Cook until soft enough to mash through ricer or sieve. If canned marrons are used, drain and mash through ricer or sieve.

Add salt, butter, cream, and sugar to chestnut purée; mix well. Beat egg yolks until thick and lemon colored, and add with brandy or sherry and vanilla extract. Blend well.

Beat egg whites until stiff but not dry. Fold into chestnut purée. Turn into an unbuttered 5-cup soufflé or casserole.

Bake in a 350° F. oven for 35 minutes or until center springs back when gently touched with finger. Serve immediately.

Makes about 6 servings.

LET'S HAVE A TEA PARTY

From the time the "tea-smitten ladies" of Holland with their magnificently appointed tea tables started to entertain guests between two and three each afternoon, and continuing on to the time when the Duchess of Bedford instituted the custom of five o'clock tea in Great Britain to alleviate her hunger pangs between breakfast and dinner, we have established a code of tea manners and customs which endures to the present day.

Nothing is as charming to the eye or to the palate as a correctly organized tea party.

Tea parties fall into five categories: the nursery tea, the informal tea, the formal tea, the tea reception, and the "high tea." The differences among them lie in the atmosphere created by the hostess, the setting of the table and tray, and the menu selected for the occasion.

An assortment of three different types of tea food should *always* be offered at teatime, all of which, with few exceptions, should be eaten with the fingers. Guests should have a choice of (1) something hot in the way of breads such as muffins, sweet rolls, and toasts; (2) something fresh and bland such as sandwiches of water cress, cucumber, or just plain bread and butter; and (3) something sweet. Barring the case of the tea reception, the tea *must* in every case be poured by the hostess or by intimate friends chosen by her.

Certain household accouterments are necessary if one is to

give a proper tea party. One is an assortment of attractive linens to cover the tea table. At informal or nursery teas the hostess may introduce a touch of whimsy; but for the formal tea and tea reception hand-rolled cloths of damask or fine batiste or linen, embroidered or appliquéd with lace, are in the best taste. Tea cloths of this type may be accompanied by six, eight, or twelve matching napkins. *The tea tray is never covered with a cloth.* The other prerequisite is, of course, the tea set.

According to tradition, there are two types of tea-tray arrangements which are equally correct. Foremost is the silver tea set made up of teapot, hot-water kettle, sugar bowl, cream pitcher, and a bowl into which the hostess can empty the dregs of the teacups should guests wish additional tea. Cups, saucers, and tea plates of china are used with the silver tea set. The second type of tea set (one which the hostess may prefer) is a tea service made of china, complete except for a silver or copper hot-water kettle. If the hostess does not possess a complete china tea set, she may combine two patterns: cups, saucers, and tea plates of one design and a tea-tray set of another design which is more decorative and ornate than the first. Thus the china given to the guests will be all of one kind.

With these appointments on hand the hostess is ready to plan her party. Let us then examine in detail each of the different styles of entertaining she may choose.

The Nursery Tea

The nursery tea is most suitable for an informal tea party in the country, for tea out-of-doors anywhere, or for any tea where children are present.

Nursery tea is always served at a big table, with all the participants grouped around on chairs. The table is covered with a sturdy, family-style cloth, and paper napkins may be used. The tea service is earthenware rather than silver or porcelain, and the tea tray may be made of brightly painted wood, shiny metal, or silver. At the opposite end of the table from the tea tray, one may place a tray holding a pitcher of milk and some tall glasses.

The tea foods are arranged in the center of the table. There should be lots of jam and honey and peanut butter (a strictly American touch) and a hefty supply of fresh bread. Butter is served at the nursery tea table but never at other teas, since ordinarily for those occasions everything requiring butter has been previously prepared in the kitchen before being offered to the guests. There is a marked absence of delicate foods at the nursery tea. Everything should be hearty. Instead of sweets there should be platters piled high with ginger snaps, oatmeal cookies, spongecake, and chocolate-chip wafers. Big cupcakes are appreciated. There should be bowls filled with whatever fruits are in season and powdered sugar as a dip for berries. The accent should always be on a plentiful variety of simple foods, the kind of snacks which lend an atmosphere of relaxed good will to the festivities.

The Informal Tea

An informal tea is the ideal way to entertain friends or group of neighbors in a gracious way. Moreover, it is economical and easy to prepare.

Tea is generally served by the hostess from a small table in the living room. The guests are invited for the hours between three and five in the afternoon and sit about the living room in groups. The tea tray is brought to the table, holding the tea service, a plate of lemon slices, the cups, saucers, tea-spoons, and napkins. The tea foods can be set on the tea tray, if there is room enough, or on the tea table next to the tea plates. If there are more than a few guests, the tea snacks can be placed on a larger table nearby or served from the traditional English three-tiered table, which can be carried conveniently among the guests. The hostess pours the tea, offering each guest a choice of milk, lemon, or sugar. When all the tea is served, the foods, which should be simple and easy to handle, are passed and guests are encouraged to serve themselves. The snacks should consist of a first course of tiny biscuits filled with marmalade or jam, tiny doughnuts, rusks, quartered muffins, French toast, cinnamon toast, scones, crescents or brioches—all served very buttery and very hot. The second course should contain tea sandwiches with fillings such as egg and anchovy, cream cheese and chopped olives, water cress and butter, pâté de foie gras, cucumber, and tomato, or thin slices of white bread rolled with cheese, toasted until the cheese is slightly melted. The most important thing to remember is that these sandwiches, which can be made prettier with a cookie cutter, *must* be small enough to afford the guest only two or three bites. Plain bread-and-butter sandwiches are very much in order for this second course. For the third course there should be a choice of delicious fresh finger fruits dipped in powdered sugar as well as a whole range of fancy cookies, small cakes, and candies.

The Formal Tea

The formal tea is one of the most versatile ways to entertain a large group. It is usually a stand-up affair, and the refreshments and tea are served from the dining room table to guests who circulate and socialize in the living and family rooms. The tea table is set with the tea service at one end and a companion service for coffee, chocolate, or punch at the other. The tea tray holds the teapot, containing the tea concentrate, a kettle of hot water, sugar, milk, and lemon. Cups and saucers are generally placed to the left of the tea tray with spoons nearby. Plates, each arranged with a napkin placed carefully on top, are set along the edge of the table, and the platters of food are arranged down the center of the table. Flowers and candles are the traditional centerpiece unless the tea celebrates an engagement, wedding, graduation, or birthday, in which case an elaborately decorated cake may serve the same purpose.

At the formal tea the hostess does not serve the tea but frees herself to greet the guests by asking two of her friends to "pour." She might also arrange for several other friends to replenish the tea foods and beverages if she does not have servants. Food for a formal tea may be much the same as for the informal tea or it may be more elegant. The hot course may include tiny sausage rolls, cheese straws, asparagus rolls, toasted cheese-and-bacon fingers, raisin tea buns, small biscuits filled with hot chicken, crab meat, shrimp, or lobster. The sandwiches may be either open-face or closed. Thin slices of white meat of chicken, minced ham and mustard relish, chopped curried egg, tuna fish with capers, cream cheese and candied ginger, toasted almonds, stuffed olives, spreads of pâté, lobster, shrimp, and liver sausage all make good fillings. The rich cakes might match the color scheme and take the form of cookies, cake fingers, tiny tarts, small frosted cupcakes, or petits fours.

Guests at the formal tea are at liberty to pull chairs up to the tea table if they so desire, but they should vacate their places as soon as possible for other guests who may also wish to enjoy their tea in this fashion. It is correct to use little individual tea tables at a formal tea but, like the main table, they should be covered with cloths.

The Tea Reception

The tea reception may replace the coming-out party, wedding reception, or even a ball if there is music for dancing. It is an excellent manner in which to fête an important personage. Because it is generally an occasion attended by an exceedingly large number of people, the food is more limited to those things which can be readily eaten when passed by servants and should include only those foods which will retain their complete flavor when left exposed on the tray. The tea table should be covered with the most handsome cloth the hostess possesses, and candles and flowers should be used to decorate the center of the reception table. The tea set is placed at one end of the table as at the formal tea, and it is balanced by a companion beverage placed at the other end. When setting the reception tea table the hostess should make a special effort to see that the cups, saucers, silverware, napkins, and tea-food platters are all symmetrically and formally arranged. She should strive for the effect of a definite design. If there are more than a hundred guests to be served, the tea may be poured in advance and offered by a butler followed by a footman or waitress who offers milk, lemon, and sugar.

In warm weather the tea tray may be arranged with a big bowl of ice, tall glasses filled with ice cubes, tea, and mint. There should also be a pitcher containing an extra supply of cold tea. (Note: Do not put iced tea in the refrigerator as refrigeration may tend to cloud it. Cloudiness doesn't affect the tea's taste at all, but it is unnecessary to put the tea in the refrigerator when it won't lose a bit of its flavor or freshness when kept for several hours at room temperature.) In combination with the warm-weather iced-tea tray setting, beverages such as fruit juices, ginger ale, lemonade, orangeade, or soft drinks might be arranged at the other end of the tea table.

Tea reception foods are much the same as those presented at the formal tea. However, American tradition demands that the third or "rich" course be a big chocolate or devil's food cake, a seven-layer cake with dark chocolate filling and frosting on top, a rich fresh coconut cake, and only the very sweetest of cookies such as chocolate leaves. In addition, salads, ices, or ice creams are often part of the tea reception menu. There should be salted nuts, mints, and bonbons in convenient places so that the guests can help themselves.

In extremely warm weather the first course of hot-tea foods is generally eliminated in favor of a larger variety of tea sandwiches and canapés and, since on hot days heavy cake may be unappetizing, very sweet finger cakes may replace the traditional chocolate delights.

The "High Tea"

At high tea or, as it is sometimes called, "meat tea," the foods are of a much heartier nature. The tea is brought out on the tray as always, but it is served between five and six and frequently replaces the evening meal. The menu differs little from that of the American buffet supper. There are hot breads, sandwiches, little grilled sausages, grilled sardines on toast, tiny codfish balls, chicken livers wrapped in bacon, and large amounts of cake and cookies. Generally at a high tea strawberries, cherries, and grapes replace the candies offered at other teas.

Thus far there has been no discussion of the most important ingredient in the tea party—the tea itself and how it ought to be made. A completely unfounded rumor is abroad which claims that only the initiated know how to make a *real* cup of tea. It is sheer nonsense to assume that the proper brewing of this beverage is a difficult ritual which only a chosen few can master. Every hostess can be an expert by following the Golden Rules for the Making of Perfect Tea. Here they are!

Golden Rules for the Making of Perfect Tea

1. Warm the teapot by filling it with hot water and emptying it just before using.
2. *Loose Tea:* Put into the teapot 1 teaspoon of tea for each cup of tea desired plus 1 teaspoon of tea for the pot.

Tea Bags: Put into the teapot 1 tea bag for each cup of tea desired.

Instant Tea: Put into the teapot or teacup 1 level teaspoon of instant tea for each cup desired.

3. Bring fresh cold tap water to a full rolling boil and add to the tea.

4. Brew 3 to 5 minutes, *by the clock,* depending on the strength you like. It takes time for the leaves to unfold and release their flavor, so don't guess. (Instant tea requires no timing because it is ready-brewed and dissolves instantly in hot or cold water.)

Hot Tea for a Crowd (concentrate for 40–45 cups; double the recipe for 85–90 cups)

Bring 1½ quarts of fresh cold water to a full rolling boil. Remove from heat. Immediately add ¼ pound loose tea. Stir to immerse leaves. Cover. Brew 5 minutes. Strain liquor into teapot until ready to use. To serve hot tea, pour 1 ounce of the tea concentrate into each cup. Add freshly made piping-hot water, varying the strength of the tea by varying the amount of concentrate you use.

Iced Tea for a Crowd (1 gallon or 20 servings)

Pour 1 quart of boiling water over 2 ounces of tea (about ⅔ cup). Brew for six minutes. Stir and strain into 3 quarts of cold tap water. Serve over ice cubes.

Note: For larger quantities simply multiply the amounts given above by the number of gallons you desire.

Iced Tea . . . the Instant Way

Iced tea can be had in seconds when using instant tea. It is not necessary to boil the water as the soluble powder dissolves instantly even in cold tap water. Just follow the directions on the jar, stir, add ice, and serve. For each single serving, use 1 rounded teapoon for a glass of 6 ounces of cold water. For a pitcherful, use about 2 tablespoons of instant tea for each quart of cold water. For a crowd, 1 small jar of instant tea will make from 1½ to 2 gallons of iced tea, depending on the strength desired.

The tea party is by far the simplest and least expensive way to entertain all the people who are important to you in personal, business, and community life, as well as your family. In perfect taste for any occasion, the tea party is easy to plan in advance and permits the hostess freedom to mingle and chat with her guests in the relaxed way that always leads to perfect success in entertaining.

TEA PARTY SANDWICHES

ASPARAGUS ROLL-UPS

24 (3½-inch) cooked
   green asparagus tips,
   drained
¼ cup French dressing

24 slices enriched bread
¾ cup Roquefort cheese
   spread
Dash of paprika

Marinate asparagus in French dressing.

Spread bread slices with cheese spread. Sprinkle with paprika. Trim crusts from bread. Place bread slices in colander with cheese side up, in a single layer.

Stand colander over boiling water, but do not allow water to touch bread. Steam bread until it just begins to feel moist on under side. Remove bread from colander.

Place an asparagus tip on top of cheese at one end of each bread slice and immediately roll up like a jelly roll.

Place on a cookie sheet so that roll rests on last turn of bread. Toast under medium broiler heat for 3 minutes, or until golden brown.

Makes 24 roll-ups.

APPLE RINGS

24 slices enriched-
   bread toast
½ cup soft butter or
   margarine
24 slices bacon, chopped

24 small slices cored
   apple, ½ inch thick
¾ pound process Ameri-
   can cheese, grated

Cut each slice of toast into a 3-inch circle with a cookie cutter.
Butter toast rounds.

Fry chopped bacon until crisp.

Sauté apple slices on both sides in bacon fat. Place apple
slices on toast rounds.

Combine bacon with cheese and sprinkle over apple.

Place on a greased cookie sheet and toast under medium
broiler heat for 2 minutes, or until cheese melts.

Makes 24 rings.

CURRANT JELLY PUFFLES

12 slices enriched-bread toast
1 egg white
3 tablespoons currant jelly

Cut each slice of toast into 4 1½-inch circles with a cookie
cutter.

Beat egg white until it begins to stiffen. Add jelly and
continue beating until mixture holds a stiff peak.

Pile about a teaspoon of meringue on each toast round.

Place on a greased cookie sheet and brown in a 400° F. oven
for 5 minutes, or until lightly browned.

Makes 48 puffles.

CHEESE CHUNKIES

1 loaf (1 pound)
    unsliced enriched
    bread
⅓ pound process American cheese

⅓ cup melted butter
    or margarine
1 teaspoon paprika

Remove crusts from bread and cut it crosswise into 6 1½-inch equal-sized slices. Cut each slice into 4 equal-sized chunks.

Cut cheese into ½-inch slices. Cut cheese slice into ½x1-inch sticks.

Hollow out part of the center of each bread chunk with scissors. Insert a cheese stick in each bread chunk. Brush with melted butter. Sprinkle paprika on top.

Place on a greased cookie sheet and toast in a 400° F. oven for 5 minutes.

Makes 24 chunkies.

CRANBERRY CINNAMON ROLLS

12 slices enriched bread
2 tablespoons soft butter
    or margarine
½ cup crushed jellied
    cranberry sauce

¼ cup melted butter
    or margarine
3 tablespoons cinnamon
    sugar

Trim crusts from bread.

Spread slices with soft butter or margarine and cranberry sauce. Roll each slice up like a jelly roll and fasten with a toothpick, if necessary. Brush rolls with melted butter and roll in cinnamon sugar.

Place on a cookie sheet so that rolls rest on last turn of bread. Toast under medium broiler heat for 3 minutes, or until golden brown.

To serve: Cut each roll in half.

Makes 24 rolls.

EAST INDIAN TIDBITS

¾ cup chopped cooked
   chicken
⅓ cup chutney, chopped
¼ teaspoon curry powder

⅔ cup mayonnaise or
   salad dressing
6 slices enriched bread

Combine chicken, chopped chutney, curry powder, and 3 tablespoons mayonnaise. Spread 3 tablespoons chicken mixture on each slice of bread.

Trim crusts from slices and cut crosswise into 4 equal-sized strips. Put a teaspoon of mayonnaise along top of each tidbit. Place on a greased cookie sheet and heat in a 400° F. oven for 5 minutes.

Makes 24 tidbits.

RAISIN-PEANUT BUTTER PINWHEEL SANDWICHES

¾ cup peanut butter
6 tablespoons chopped,
   seedless raisins
6 tablespoons orange
   juice

2 lengthwise thin slices
   enriched bread (cut
   from unsliced sandwich
   loaf)

Combine peanut butter, raisins, and orange juice.

Spread ½ cup raisin-peanut-butter mixture on each slice of bread. Cut each slice into crosswise equal halves.

Roll each half slice of bread up like a jelly roll. Wrap each roll in waxed paper, twisting ends of paper. Place on a flat surface so that roll rests on last turn of bread; chill.

To serve: unwrap and cut each roll into 6 slices.

Makes 24 sandwiches.

ROQUEFORT-VEGETABLE POCKETBOOK SANDWICHES

¾ cup chopped cabbage
½ teaspoon chopped green pepper
2 tablespoons chopped celery
2 tablespoons mayonnaise or salad dressing

1 tablespoon crumbled Roquefort cheese
2 lengthwise slices whole wheat bread (cut from unsliced 1½-pound loaf)
¼ cup soft butter or margarine

Combine cabbage, green pepper, celery, mayonnaise, and cheese.

Spread each slice of bread with butter. Spread half of the Roquefort-vegetable filling over each slice.

Cut each lengthwise slice into 4 crosswise sections. Roll each section up tightly as for jelly roll, using a small spatula as you roll sandwiches to keep the filling from spreading out. Fasten end of sandwich with whole clove for pocketbook effect.

Wrap in waxed paper and place on a cookie sheet so that roll rests on last turn of bread. Chill until ready to serve.

Makes 8 sandwiches.

SHRIMP CRESCENTS

¼ cup cooked, finely
chopped shrimp
¼ cup finely chopped
celery
⅛ cup mayonnaise or
salad dressing

2 teaspoons lemon juice
6 slices enriched bread
1 tablespoon soft butter
or margarine

Combine shrimp, celery, mayonnaise, and lemon juice.

Spread each slice of bread with butter or margarine. Cut each slice of bread into 4 crescents with a cookie cutter.

Spread 1 teaspoon shrimp mixture on each crescent.

Garnish if desired.

Makes 24 crescents.

AVOCADO-PINEAPPLE TEA SANDWICHES

1 medium avocado,
mashed
¼ cup drained, crushed
pineapple
2 teaspoons lemon juice

2 tablespoons mayonnaise
or salad dressing
8 slices whole wheat
bread
16 tiny pieces of green
pepper

Combine mashed avocado, pineapple, lemon juice, and mayonnaise.

Cut each slice of bread into 4 1½-inch circles with a cookie cutter.

Spread each circle with 1 teaspoon avocado mixture.

Garnish if desired.

Makes 48 sandwiches.

CREAM CHEESE-JELLY CUBE SANDWICHES

36 cubes (1 inch square)
enriched bread
1 package (3 ounces)
cream cheese

1 tablespoon milk
3 tablespoons fruit jelly
or preserves

Pull part of the center out of each bread cube with a pair of tweezers.

Combine cream cheese and milk.

Spread cream cheese over the sides and top rim of each cube. Place ¼ teaspoon jelly in the center of each cube.

Makes 36 sandwiches.

CREAM CHEESE-DEVILED HAM RIBBON SANDWICHES

1 can (3 ounces)
deviled ham
1 package (3 ounces)
cream cheese
6 slices enriched bread

3 slices whole wheat
bread
3 tablespoons soft
butter or margarine

Combine deviled ham and cream cheese.

Spread bread with butter. Cover 3 slices enriched bread with ham mixture and a slice of whole wheat bread. Spread whole wheat bread with ham mixture and top with a second slice of enriched bread.

Cut crusts off and wrap in waxed paper. Chill.

To serve: Unwrap and cut sandwich into 5 sections.

Makes 15 sandwiches.

DEVILED EGG FLOWERPOTS

8 hard-cooked egg yolks
¼ cup mayonnaise or
  salad dressing
2 teaspoons vinegar
2 teaspoons Worcester-
  shire sauce
2 teaspoons prepared
  mustard

1 teaspoon grated onion
Dash of salt
8 1-inch-thick slices
  bread
32 small radish roses
32 small parsley leaves

To make filling: Mash egg yolks; add mayonnaise, vinegar, Worcestershire sauce, mustard, onion, and salt. With a 1½-inch cookie cutter, cut out 4 circles from each slice of bread. Hollow out part of the center of each bread circle with scissors.

Fill center of each bread circle with 1½ teaspoons deviled egg filling.

Garnish top of flowerpot with a radish rose and a parsley leaf.

Makes 32 Deviled Egg Flowerpots.

PINEAPPLE CHEESE FLOWERPOTS

1 package (3 ounces)
  cream cheese
⅓ cup drained, crushed
  pineapple

6 1-inch-thick slices
  bread
24 fresh strawberries
24 small parsley leaves

To make filling: Combine cream cheese and pineapple.
  Remove crusts from bread and cut each slice into 4 equal

squares. Hollow out part of the center of each bread square with scissors.

Fill center and top of each bread square with 1½ teaspoons pineapple cheese filling.

Make crosswise cuts in the pointed top of each strawberry and spread them open like flowers. Garnish top of each flowerpot with a strawberry flower and a parsley leaf.

Makes 24 Pineapple Cheese Flowerpots.

RAINBOW BARS

6 slices enriched bread
3 slices wheat bread
3 tablespoons soft butter
  or margarine

¾ cup ham-pickle filling
¾ cup ripe-olive-egg filling

Spread each slice of bread with butter.

Spread ¼ cup ham-pickle filling on 3 slices buttered enriched bread and top with wheat bread, buttered side up.

Spread ¼ cup egg-olive filling on wheat bread and top with another slice of enriched bread, buttered side down.

Press sandwich together firmly, cut off crusts and wrap each sandwich in waxed paper; chill.

To serve: Unwrap and cut crosswise into 5 slices. Cut each slice in half.

Makes 30 Rainbow Bars.

OPEN-FACE SANDWICHES

12 lengthwise slices
enriched bread (cut
from unsliced 1½
pound loaves)
¼ cup soft butter or
margarine
1 cup pineapple-ham
filling

1 cup egg-cheese salad
filling
5 slices jellied cranberry
sauce
12 radish slices, halved
12 cucumber slices, halved

Using a 2-inch rotary cookie wheel, or individual cookie cutters, make 4 or more cutouts from each slice of bread.

Spread ¼ teaspoon butter on each cutout, then spread half of them with 2 teaspoons pineapple-ham filling and half of them with 2 teaspoons egg-cheese filling. Cut cranberry sauce slices into 24 fancy shapes with tiny hors d'oeuvres cutters.

Cut radish and cucumber slices in half.

Garnish pineapple-ham sandwiches with a cranberry cutout and egg-cheese sandwiches with a halved cucumber and radish slice.

Makes 24 egg-cheese open-face sandwiches and 24 pineapple-ham open-face sandwiches.

PINEAPPLE-HAM FILLING

1 cup ground, cooked ham
¼ cup drained, crushed
pineapple
1 tablespoon brown sugar
1 tablespoon mayonnaise
or salad dressing

1 tablespoon prepared
horseradish
½ teaspoon Worcester-
shire sauce

Combine ham, pineapple, brown sugar, mayonnaise, horse-radish, and Worcestershire sauce.

Makes 1 cup.

EGG-CHEESE SANDWICH FILLING

½ cup chopped hard-cooked eggs
1 cup grated process American cheese
3 tablespoons mayon-naise or salad dressing

½ teaspoon vinegar
2 teaspoons grated onion
½ teaspoon prepared mustard
⅛ teaspoon salt

Combine eggs, cheese, mayonnaise, vinegar, onion, mustard, and salt.

Makes 1 cup.

CHEESE-BACON RYETTES

½ cup sharp cheese spread
2 tablespoons chopped, cooked bacon

24 thin slices party rye bread
24 stuffed olive slices
24 watercress leaves

Combine cheese spread and bacon.
   Spread on each slice of rye bread, using 1 teaspoon cheese-bacon mixture per slice.
   Garnish each one with an olive slice and watercress leaf.

Makes 24 Cheese-Bacon Ryettes.

HAM-PICKLE SANDWICH FILLING

⅔ cup chopped cooked
   ham
2 tablespoons chopped
   dill pickle

3 tablespoons mayon-
   naise or salad dressing

Combine ham, dill pickle, and mayonnaise.

Makes ¾ cup or filling for 4 sandwiches.

RIPE-OLIVE-EGG SANDWICH FILLING

¾ cup chopped hard-
   cooked eggs
2 tablespoons chopped
   ripe olives

1 tablespoon chopped
   green pepper
½ teaspoon salt
2 tablespoons mayonnaise
   or salad dressing

Combine eggs, olives, green pepper, salt, and mayonnaise.

Makes ¾ cup or filling for 4 sandwiches.

ASSORTED OBLETS

1 package (3 ounces)
   cream cheese
2 tablespoons milk
12 slices enriched bread
4 teaspoons soft butter
   or margarine
6 tablespoons currant
   jelly

6 tablespoons peanut
   butter
6 tablespoons sharp
   cheese spread
½ cup toasted shredded
   coconut
½ cup finely chopped nuts

Soften cream cheese with milk.

Make 6 sandwiches, 2 each of jelly, peanut butter, and sharp cheese. Use 3 tablespoons of filling for each kind of sandwich. Butter the bread used for jelly sandwiches.

Spread softened cream cheese over top of each sandwich. Trim crusts. To cut, slice each sandwich in half crosswise, and divide each half into 3 oblong sections.

To garnish top of oblets, dip half of them into toasted coconut and other half into chopped nuts.

Makes 36 Assorted Oblets.

CHEESE ANGLES

1¾ cups or 7 ounces
 grated sharp cheese,
 firmly packed
¼ cup chopped stuffed
 olives
¼ cup or 1 can (2¼
 ounces) deviled ham

2 teaspoons prepared
 mustard
¼ cup mayonnaise or
 salad dressing
1 loaf (1 pound) un-
 sliced enriched bread
1 loaf (1 pound) un-
 sliced wheat bread

To make filling: Combine cheese, olives, ham, mustard, and mayonnaise.

Remove crusts from each loaf of bread, making both loaves equal in size. Divide each loaf in half by making a lengthwise diagonal cut to form two triangles. Place the widest side of each triangle down on the breadboard. Slice each triangle lengthwise from the pointed ridge down through the center of the base, making 8 long bread triangles.

Spread one side of each bread triangle with 3 tablespoons filling.

Reassemble into 2 loaves by alternating 2 triangles of each

kind of bread per loaf. Press together and wrap each loaf in waxed paper; chill.

To serve: Unwrap and cut each loaf into 15 slices. Cut each slice in half.

Makes 60 Cheese Angles.

CHERRY CHEESE WHEELS

1 package (3 ounces) cream cheese

2 tablespoons chopped maraschino cherries

2 lengthwise thin slices enriched bread (cut from unsliced sandwich loaf)

2 tablespoons soft butter or margarine

16 maraschino cherries

Combine cream cheese and chopped cherries.

Trim crusts from lengthwise bread slices. Spread each slice of bread with butter, then with cheese-cherry mixture.

Cut each slice in equal halves crosswise. Place a row of four cherries across one of the narrow edges of each half slice of bread, pressing cherries firmly together end to end.

Roll each half slice of bread as for jelly roll, starting at cherry end, being careful to keep cherries firmly in place. Wrap each roll in waxed paper, twisting ends of paper. Place on flat surface so that roll rests on last turn of bread; chill.

To serve: Unwrap and cut each roll into 6 slices.

Makes 24 wheels.

ROLL-UP AND PINWHEEL SANDWICHES

Step 1. Trim crusts from bread.

Step 2. Roll bread with rolling pin.

Step 3. Cover slice with the spread. Place ingredients at one end.

Step 4. Roll up carefully and wrap in foil or waxed paper.

Step 5. Twist ends of foil or waxed paper to seal and refrigerate.

FOR ROLL-UP SANDWICHES:
Slices may be spread with butter, margarine, cream cheese, or jam. Use cooked asparagus spears, stuffed celery, or other filling of your choice. For added color try a sprig of water cress at one end.

FOR PINWHEEL SANDWICHES:
Use red or green cherries, Vienna or cocktail franks, gherkins, pitted dates, or pitted olives. Make roll-up sandwiches as described above. Slice into circular discs about ½ inch thick with serrated knife through the foil or waxed paper.

RIBBON SANDWICHES

(May be made with 3 or more slices, always alternating dark and white bread.)

Step 1. Spread 2 slices of bread (1 white, 1 dark) with butter or cream cheese, jam or salad spread, and press together. Spread top side and add another slice of alternate color. Press together to form 3 slices.

Step 2. Wrap in foil or waxed paper and refrigerate for an hour or more. (This makes the sandwich firm and easier to handle.)

Step 3. Firmly but gently press down on stack and trim crusts from all 4 sides using a sharp knife and a sawing motion. Cut into ½-inch to ¾-inch slices.

Step 4. If you wish, cut each ribbon into thirds, halves, or triangles.

CHECKERBOARDS

(As with ribbon sandwiches, always alternate the white and dark slices.)

Step 1. Alternate 2 dark and 2 white slices. Spread both sides with butter, cream cheese, or jam except the top and bottom outside slices.

Step 2. Cut into ribbons (as described before). Spread with butter, cream cheese, or jam and reverse ribbons to form checkerboard pattern.

Step 3. Even out and press ribbons to form checkerboard loaf. Wrap in foil or waxed paper and refrigerate for an hour or more. Cut with sharp knife into ½-inch to ¾-inch slices.

TEA PARTY CAKES

ORANGE BLOSSOM CAKE

1 cup milk
½ cup sugar
1 teaspoon salt
½ cup butter or
  margarine
½ cup very warm water
3 packages or cakes yeast,
  active dry or com-
  pressed

3 eggs, beaten
6½ to 7 cups sifted all-
  purpose flour
½ cup sugar
½ cup chopped pecans
¼ cup grated orange rind
½ cup orange juice

Scald milk; stir in sugar, salt, and margarine. Cool to lukewarm.

Measure very warm water into bowl. Sprinkle or crumble
in yeast; stir until dissolved. Stir in lukewarm milk mixture,
eggs, and half the flour. Beat until smooth. Stir in enough
remaining flour to make a soft dough. Turn out on a lightly
floured board and knead until smooth and elastic.

Divide dough in half. Roll each half into a rope 16 inches
long. Cut each into 16 equal pieces. Shape into balls. Place
balls in well-greased 10-inch tube pan. Brush lightly with

melted butter. Sprinkle with half the mixture of sugar, pecans, and orange rind. Repeat with remaining balls, and sugar mixture.

Cover and let rise in warm place, free from draft, until doubled in bulk, about 45 minutes.

Bake in a 350° F. oven 40 to 45 minutes. Let cool in a pan on wire rack 10 minutes. Invert pan and finish cooling. Remove cake. Pierce sides and bottom with tines of fork and spoon on orange juice until absorbed.

Makes 1 10-inch cake.

CINNAMON CAKE

1¼ cups sifted all-purpose flour
2½ teaspoons double-acting baking powder
1 teaspoon ground cinnamon
¼ teaspoon salt
⅓ cup vegetable shortening

1 cup sugar
2 eggs
½ cup milk
1 tablespoon butter or margarine, melted
1 tablespoon sugar
¼ teaspoon ground cinnamon

Sift first 4 ingredients together. Set aside for later use.

Cream shortening and sugar together. Beat in eggs, one at a time. Add flour mixture alternately with milk. Beat ½ minute.

Pour into a well-greased, lightly floured 8x8x2-inch pan. Bake 60 minutes or until done in a 350° F. oven. Turn out pan onto cooling rack.

Brush top with melted butter or margarine. Combine sugar and cinnamon and sprinkle over cake.

Makes 1 cake.

CHOCOLATE FILBERT CAKE

2¾ cups sifted cake flour
2 teaspoons baking
   powder
½ teaspoon salt
1 cup butter or
   margarine
1⅔ cups sugar
4 egg yolks, unbeaten

1 package (4 ounces)
   sweet chocolate,
   melted and cooled
1 teaspoon pure vanilla
   extract
1 cup milk
1 cup finely chopped
   filberts or walnuts
4 egg whites

Sift flour, baking powder, and salt together. Cream butter or margarine, add sugar gradually, and beat until light and fluffy. Add egg yolks, one at a time, beating well after each. Blend in melted chocolate and vanilla.

Add flour mixture alternately with milk, beating well after each addition. Fold in nuts. Beat egg whites until stiff peaks form and fold into batter.

Pour into a well-greased and floured 10-inch tube pan or a 13x9x2-inch pan. Bake in a 350° F. oven 1 hour and 10 to 15 minutes for tube pan, or 50 to 55 minutes for 13x9x2-inch pan. Cool 15 minutes; then remove from pan. Cool on rack. Spread Broiled Coconut Topping on oblong cake and broil until lightly browned and bubbly, about 3 minutes. Serve tube cake plain or with ice cream.

Broiled Coconut Topping: Melt ½ cup butter. Add 1 cup firmly packed brown sugar, 1⅓ cups flake coconut, and ⅓ cup light cream. Mix well. Let stand about 3 minutes.

SPONGECAKE

6 egg whites (¾ cup)
1 teaspoon cream of
tartar
1½ cups sifted sugar
1⅓ cups sifted cake flour

½ teaspoon baking
powder
½ teaspoon salt
6 egg yolks (½ cup)
¼ cup water
1 teaspoon lemon extract

Combine egg whites and cream of tartar in large bowl. Beat until soft mounds begin to form. (Beat at high speed of electric beater or use sturdy egg beater or flat wire whip.) Add ½ cup of the sugar gradually, 2 tablespoons at a time, and continue beating until very stiff peaks are formed. (Do not underbeat.)

Sift flour, baking powder, salt, and remaining 1 cup of the sugar into small bowl. Add egg yolks, water, and lemon extract; beat with spoon just until blended (about 75 strokes). Carefully fold into beaten egg whites, using about 30 fold-over strokes.

Pour batter into ungreased 10-inch tube pan. Cut gently through batter to remove large air bubbles. Bake in 375° F. oven about 35 minutes. Remove from oven. Cool cake in pan, upside down, 1 or 2 hours. Then loosen from sides and center tube with knife and gently remove cake.

Chocolate Apricot Torte: Prepare spongecake as directed. Pour batter into three 8-inch ungreased layer pans. Bake in 375° F. oven about 15 minutes. Cool upside down in pans about 1 hour. Split each layer to make 6 thin layers. Spread apricot jam thinly between layers, using about 1¼ cups jam. Spread Easy Chocolate Frosting on top and sides of cake.

EASY CHOCOLATE FROSTING

4 squares unsweetened
  chocolate
¼ cup butter or
  margarine
1 pound sifted confec-
  tioners' sugar

⅛ teaspoon salt
½ cup milk
1 teaspoon pure vanilla
  extract

Melt chocolate and butter or margarine over hot water. Blend sugar, salt, milk, and vanilla. Add chocolate mixture. Let stand, stirring occasionally until of spreading consistency.

Makes 2½ cups frosting.

FRENCH CHOCOLATE CAKE

2½ squares unsweetened
  chocolate, coarsely
  chopped
¾ cup boiling water
½ teaspoon soda
½ cup sour cream
2 cups sifted cake flour

¼ teaspoon salt
⅓ cup butter or
  margarine
1½ cups sugar
1 teaspoon pure vanilla
  extract
3 egg whites

Melt chocolate in the boiling water; cool to room temperature. Dissolve soda in the sour cream and set aside.

Sift flour and salt together. Cream butter, add sugar gradually, and cream together until light and fluffy. Add chocolate mixture and vanilla; beat well. Blend in the sour-cream mixture. Then add flour, ¼ at a time, beating after each addition until smooth. Beat egg whites until soft peaks form; fold into the batter.

Pour batter into 13x9x2-inch pan which has been lined on bottom with paper. Bake in a 325° F. oven 35 minutes. Cool cake, cut in half, and split each half, making 4 thin layers. Spread Chocolate Butter Frosting thinly between layers and on top and sides of cake. Spread Bittersweet Chocolate Coating over frosting on sides of cake and pour over top of cake in 3 thin straight lines. Draw toothpick through lines of chocolate at right angles, keeping strokes an even distance apart.

BUTTER CHOCOLATE FROSTING

⅔ cup butter or margarine
⅛ teaspoon salt
1½ cups sifted confec-
  tioners' sugar

6 egg yolks, unbeaten
4 squares unsweetened
  chocolate, melted and
  cooled

Cream butter and salt until butter is soft. Gradually add the sugar, beating after each addition until light and fluffy. Add the egg yolks, one at a time, beating well after each. Then add the cooled chocolate slowly, blending well.

Makes about 2 cups.

Bittersweet Chocolate Coating: Melt 2 squares unsweetened chocolate with 2 teaspoons butter over hot water. Pour coating over frosting in desired pattern.

CINNAMON STREUSSEL TEACAKE

2 cups sifted all-purpose flour
3 teaspoons baking powder
1 teaspoon salt
½ cup sugar
1 teaspoon ground cinnamon
⅓ cup vegetable shortening
1 egg, well beaten

½ cup milk
Melted butter or margarine

TOPPING:
2 tablespoons all-purpose flour
2 tablespoons butter or margarine
5 tablespoons sugar
¾ teaspoon ground cinnamon

Sift the 2 cups flour, baking powder, salt, the ½ cup sugar, and the 1 teaspoon cinnamon into a large mixing bowl. Cut in shortening until mixture resembles coarse cornmeal.

Add milk to egg and stir into dry ingredients just until mixed.

Spread in a greased 8x8x2-inch pan. Brush with melted butter or margarine.

Combine remaining ingredients until they form a crumbly mixture. Sprinkle over top of cake. Bake in a 400° F. oven 25 to 30 minutes or until done.

Makes 16 servings.

CINNAMON COCONUT TOSS CAKE

1 package active dry yeast
2 tablespoons lukewarm
  water
½ cup milk
2 tablespoons butter or
  margarine
2 tablespoons sugar
1 teaspoon salt

1 egg
2½ cups sifted all-purpose
  flour
2 teaspoons ground
  cinnamon
1 cup sugar
¾ cup flake coconut
1 egg, well beaten

Soften yeast in water. Let stand 5 minutes.

Scald milk and combine with butter or margarine, sugar, and salt. Cool to lukewarm. Stir in yeast and egg. Add flour gradually. Stir to form dough. Cover and let rise in a warm place (85° to 90° F.) until double in bulk, about 1 hour. Spread in a greased 13x9x2-inch pan. (The batter will be spread thinly, but do not put in a smaller pan.)

Combine remaining cinnamon, sugar, coconut, and egg. Spread over top of dough. Cover and let rise in a warm place (85° to 90° F.) until double in bulk, about 30 minutes.

Bake in a 375° F. oven until golden brown, about 30 to 35 minutes. Serve warm.

Makes 16 servings.

TEA PARTY COOKIES

CINNAMON TEA LEAVES

1 cup sifted all-purpose
  flour
½ teaspoon salt
½ teaspoon ground
  cinnamon
½ teaspoon ground
  nutmeg

⅓ cup butter or
  margarine
⅓ cup sugar
1 egg
1 teaspoon grated lemon
  rind
⅔ cup chopped walnuts

Sift together flour, salt, cinnamon, and nutmeg. Cream margarine. Add sugar and cream until light and fluffy.

Add egg, lemon rind, and walnuts; mix thoroughly.

Blend in dry ingredients. Chill 1 hour.

Shape dough into a roll about 8 inches long and 1½ inches in diameter. Wrap in foil. Chill 2 hours.

Cut chilled dough into slices ¼ inch thick. Place on ungreased baking sheet; shape with hands to resemble leaves. To mark "veins" use blunt edge of a table knife. Sprinkle with sugar. Bake in a 375° F. oven 12 to 15 minutes.

Makes 2½ dozen leaves.

SWEET BANANA PUFFS

2 cups sifted cake flour
Dash salt
½ cup butter or margarine
¼ cup buttermilk

2 ripe bananas
¼ cup shredded coconut
½ teaspoon lemon juice
Unbeaten egg white

Start heating oven to 400° F. Grease a cookie sheet. Sift flour and salt into bowl. With pastry blender or 2 knives, scissors fashion, cut in butter until mixture resembles coarse cornmeal. Add buttermilk; mix well. On lightly floured surface, knead dough a few times; then roll out to ¼-inch thickness. With floured cookie cutter, cut into 3-inch rounds.

In bowl, with fork, mash bananas; add coconut and lemon juice, then mix well. Place a teaspoonful of this mixture in the center of each round of dough. Fold each round so edges come together, then seal edges with tines of fork. Brush tops with unbeaten egg white.

Place 1 inch apart on greased cookie sheet. Bake 25 minutes or until golden brown on top.

Makes about 24 puffs.

EASTER PETITES

6 egg whites
⅛ teaspoon salt
2 cups sugar

1 cup grated semisweet
chocolate

Beat egg whites and salt until frothy. Add sugar a tablespoonful at a time, and beat until meringue is very stiff and will hold peaks. Fold in chocolate, a small amount at a time.

Cover a cookie sheet with brown paper, and using a spoon or pastry tube, shape small meringues. Bake in a 250° F. oven for 1 hour. Remove from cookie sheet when cool.

Makes about 20 small meringues.

CHEESE-FRUIT PASTIES

DOUGH:

½ cup butter or margarine softened
1 package (8 ounces) cream cheese
½ to ¾ cup Roquefort cheese, crumbled

1½ cups sifted all-purpose flour
¼ teaspoon salt
1 egg, beaten

FILLING VARIATIONS:

Jellies: orange marmalade, quince jelly, etc.
Mincemeat
Apple slices, very thin

Cream butter and cream cheese thoroughly. Blend in flour and salt. Chill several hours or overnight.

Roll dough approximately ⅛ inch thick. Cut into 3- or 4-inch rounds or squares and place on a cookie sheet. For a variety of pasties place ½–1 teaspoon Roquefort and same amount of jelly or mincemeat in center of each round or square; or spread thin apple slices with Roquefort and proceed as above. Fold over to form half moons or triangles and press edges together. Prick with a fork for a decorative touch, if desired. Brush tops with egg. Bake in a 450° F. oven 10 minutes.

Makes 36 pasties.

CARDAMOM FORK COOKIES

1 cup butter or margarine
2 teaspoons baking soda
1 teaspoon ground
cardamom
½ teaspoon salt
2 cups light brown sugar,
firmly packed

2 eggs
4½ cups sifted all-
purpose flour
2 teaspoons cream of
tartar

Soften butter or margarine, add soda, cardamom, and salt. Mix well. Gradually blend in sugar. Beat in eggs.

Sift flour with cream of tartar and gradually stir into the mixture.

Chill dough 3 to 4 hours or until stiff enough to handle. Shape into ½-inch balls. Place on ungreased cookie sheets. Dip a fork in flour and press into each cookie in crisscross style.

Bake in a 350° F. oven 10 minutes. Cool and store in a tightly closed tin box or cookie jar.

Makes approximately 8 dozen cookies.

SPICED BUTTER FINGERS

¾ cup butter or
margarine
½ teaspoon ground cloves
½ teaspoon ground ginger
½ teaspoon ground
nutmeg

⅓ cup sugar
1 cup chopped nuts
2 cups sifted all-purpose
flour
⅓ cup water

Soften butter or margarine and blend with spices. Gradually add sugar.

Stir in nuts. Add flour alternately with water.

Shape into oblong cookies about the size of one's little finger. Bake in a 350° F. oven 15 to 20 minutes.

Cool and roll in granulated sugar.

Makes 3½ dozen fingers.

SPICED SESAME SEED CRESCENTS

2½ cups sifted all-purpose flour
1 teaspoon double-acting baking powder
1½ teaspoons ground mace

¼ teaspoon salt
1 cup sugar
⅔ cup butter or margarine
1 egg, lightly beaten
Toasted sesame seed

Sift together flour, baking powder, mace, and salt. Gradually stir sugar into softened butter or margarine. Beat in egg. Add flour mixture gradually, mixing after each addition.

Let dough stand 30 minutes at room temperature.

With fingers, on waxed paper, shape a rounded teaspoon of dough at a time into a roll 2 inches long. Taper ends. Roll in lightly toasted sesame seed.

Place on an ungreased cookie sheet. Curve ends to form crescents.

Bake in a 375° F. oven 18 to 20 minutes or until lightly browned around the bottom. Cool on wire rack.

Store in a tightly closed cookie jar or box.

Makes 4 dozen crescents.

To toast sesame seed: Spread a thin layer of sesame seed in a large shallow baking pan. Toast in a 350° F. oven 20 to 22 minutes or until lightly browned.

CHUTNEY CRESCENTS

½ cup (1 stick) butter or
  margarine
1 package (3 ounces)
  cream cheese
1 cup sifted all-purpose flour

½ cup chutney
⅓ cup sugar
1 teaspoon ground
  cinnamon

Cream margarine and cream cheese until smoothly blended.
Beat in flour.

Shape dough into smooth ball; wrap in waxed paper or
aluminum foil. Chill overnight.

Remove dough from refrigerator 30 minutes before using.
Roll dough to ⅛-inch thickness; cut with 3-inch cookie cutter.
Place small spoonful of chutney in center of each round.
Fold over; press edges together. Bake on ungreased baking
sheet in moderate oven (375° F.) about 15 minutes. Roll in
sugar mixed with cinnamon.

Makes 2 dozen crescents.

CEYLON LIME WAFERS

1 cup (2 sticks) butter or
  margarine
2 cups sugar
3 eggs
1 teaspoon grated lime
  rind

3 tablespoons unstrained
  lime juice
½ teaspoon salt
¼ teaspoon ground
  ginger
5 cups sifted all-purpose
  flour

Cream margarine until light. Gradually add sugar and beat
until light and fluffy.

MARBLED TEA PUNCH CAKE. Made a day ahead, this party cake makes entertaining as easy as pouring a perfect cup of tea.

A CAKE RING. This cake is suited to every occasion and teams up deliciously with fresh fruits in season. It stores well and will keep its unique flavor and fine texture.

TEA CAKE LOAVES. These have a subtle spice flavor. Serve them with fresh fruits in season or garnished with nuts.

Add eggs, grated lime rind, lime juice, salt, and ginger; blend well.

Add enough sifted flour to make a soft dough that can be rolled out.

Roll dough on lightly floured board to ⅛-inch thickness. Cut cookies with 2-inch cutter. Place on greased baking sheet. Bake in a 375° F. oven 12 to 15 minutes.

Makes 8 dozen wafers.

SESAME TWISTS

4½ cups sifted all-purpose
   flour
2 teaspoons baking
   powder
½ teaspoon salt
1 cup (2 sticks) butter or
   margarine
1¾ cups sugar

2 eggs
⅔ cup toasted sesame
   seeds
½ teaspoon grated lemon
   rind
2 tablespoons water
2 tablespoons lemon
   juice

Sift flour, baking powder, and salt together. Cream margarine and sugar until light and fluffy. Beat in eggs, then stir in ⅓ cup toasted sesame seeds and lemon rind. Add the flour mixture alternately with the water and lemon juice.

Divide dough into 8 equal parts. Roll each into a strip 24 inches long; cut into 6 pieces. Along one side at ½-inch intervals cut slits halfway through each piece. Coil ends toward the center of uncut side. Place on greased baking sheet. Sprinkle with remaining sesame seeds.

Bake in a 400° F. oven 10 to 12 minutes.

Makes about 4 dozen twists.

COCONUT BARS

⅓ cup butter or
  margarine
1½ cups light brown
  sugar, firmly packed
1¼ cups sifted all-
  purpose flour
½ teaspoon salt

1 teaspoon pure vanilla
  extract
2 eggs
1 cup chopped pecans
1 can (3½ ounces) flaked
  coconut

Cream margarine. Add ½ cup of the sugar and cream until light and fluffy. Add 1 cup of the flour and mix well.

Pat into greased 13x9x2-inch pan. Bake in a 375° F. oven 12 minutes.

Mix together remaining sugar, flour, and remaining ingredients. Spread evenly on mixture in pan. Bake 20 minutes longer. Cut into bars. Cool. Store airtight.

Makes 4 dozen bars.

NUTMEG COCONUT ALMOND BARS

½ cup (1 stick) butter or
  margarine
1½ cups light brown sugar
1¼ cups sifted all-purpose
  flour
½ teaspoon ground
  nutmeg

½ teaspoon salt
2 large eggs, beaten
1 cup flaked coconut
1 cup chopped blanched
  almonds

Soften butter or margarine. Blend in ½ cup sugar. Add 1 cup flour and mix well.

Turn into a buttered 13x9x2-inch pan and pat the mixture uniformly over bottom.

Bake in a 375° F. oven 12 minutes. Remove from oven.

Combine remaining 1 cup sugar and ¼ cup flour, nutmeg, and salt. Mix well. Add eggs, coconut, and almonds. Spread evenly over the prebaked crust. Bake 20 minutes or until golden brown. Cool.

Cut into 24 bars. Store airtight.

Makes 2 dozen bars.

SPICED TEA BARS

1¼ cups sifted all-purpose flour
¼ teaspoon salt
1 teaspoon baking powder
½ teaspoon ground allspice
¼ teaspoon ground nutmeg
⅛ teaspoon ground cloves

½ cup vegetable shortening
½ cup light brown sugar
½ cup honey
2 eggs
1 teaspoon pure vanilla extract
½ cup chopped nuts
½ cup chopped seedless raisins

Sift the first 6 ingredients together and set aside. Cream shortening with brown sugar until fluffy. Blend in honey. Beat in eggs and vanilla extract. Stir in nuts, raisins, and sifted flour mixture. Mix well.

Spread batter in a greased, paper-lined 12x8x2-inch pan.

Bake in a 350° F. oven, 30 to 35 minutes or until done. Cool in pan 5 minutes. Turn out onto a wire rack to finish cooling. Cut into 32 bars. Store in a tightly closed cookie jar or tin box.

Makes 32 bars.

ROLLED PECAN STICKS

½ cup (1 stick) butter or
    margarine
1¼ cups sifted all-purpose
    flour

3 egg yolks
1 teaspoon grated lemon
    rind
Pecan filling

Cut margarine into the sifted flour until mixture resembles coarse meal.

Combine egg yolks and grated lemon rind; mix into flour lightly with a fork.

Divide dough into 36 pieces; shape each into a ball. Refrigerate several hours or overnight.

When ready to bake, prepare the filling (below). Roll each ball of dough out into a 3-inch circle; spread with some of the filling; roll up like a jelly roll. Place, seam side down, on an ungreased baking sheet. Bake in a 350° F. oven 15 to 20 minutes or until golden. Cool on wire racks. Sprinkle lightly with confectioners' sugar.

Makes 3 dozen sticks.

Pecan filling: Beat 3 egg whites until they stand in peaks; gradually beat in ¾ cup sugar, continuing to beat until stiff and glossy. Fold in 1½ cups chopped pecans.

TEA PARTY BREADS

VANILLA BUTTERSCOTCH BREAD

3 cups sifted all-
    purpose flour
1¼ teaspoons double-
    acting baking powder
¾ teaspoon salt
¾ teaspoon baking soda
2 eggs, beaten

1½ cups light brown sugar
⅓ cup butter or
    margarine, melted
1½ teaspoons pure vanilla
    extract
¾ cup chopped nuts
1½ cups buttermilk

Sift together the first 4 ingredients and set aside.

Beat eggs in a mixing bowl. Gradually blend in sugar. Add butter or margarine and vanilla extract. Stir in nuts. Add flour mixture alternately with milk, mixing only enough to blend the ingredients.

Turn into a well-greased, lightly floured 9x5x3-inch loaf pan. Bake in a 350° F. oven 1 hour or until done.

Cool in pan 10 minutes. Turn out onto a wire rack to finish cooling. This bread cuts better if made the day before it is to be eaten.

Serve spread with butter and marmalade, cream cheese, or peanut butter.

Makes 1 loaf.

DATE AND NUT TEA LOAF

1½ cups sifted all-
    purpose flour
½ teaspoon salt
1 teaspoon double-
    acting baking powder
1½ cups sugar
1 cup chopped pitted dates

¾ cup chopped raisins
2 cups pecans, coarsely
    chopped
2 eggs, separated
3 teaspoons pure vanilla
    extract

Sift together flour, salt, baking powder, and sugar.

Combine dates, raisins, and pecans. Add to dry ingredients and mix with fingers until well blended. Beat egg yolks with vanilla extract and add. Mix well.

Beat egg whites stiff and blend into the mixture.

Turn into a well-greased, lightly floured 9x5x3-inch loaf pan. Bake in a 300° F. oven 1 hour 30 minutes or until a cake tester inserted in center comes out clean.

Cool in pan 10 minutes. Turn out on cake rack. Cool. Wrap in foil or store in a tightly closed tin box. Keep 24 hours before serving. To serve, cut in very thin slices.

Makes 1 loaf.

CASHEW NUT AND ORANGE LOAF

2¼ cups sifted all-
    purpose flour
3½ teaspoons double-
    acting baking powder
¼ teaspoon salt
1 cup finely chopped,
    salted cashew nuts

⅔ cup sugar
⅓ cup butter or margarine
¾ cup finely chopped
    glacé orange peel
2 eggs
½ cup milk
½ cup orange juice

Sift together flour, baking powder, and salt. Add cashew nuts and set aside.

Gradually blend sugar with shortening. Add glacé orange peel and mix well. Beat in eggs, one at a time. Add flour mixture alternately with milk and orange juice.

Turn into a well-greased, lightly floured 9x5x3-inch loaf pan. Bake in a 350° F. oven 1 hour or until a cake tester inserted in the center comes out clean. Do not cut this bread until the bread is at least 1 day old. Store airtight.

Makes one 9-inch loaf.

BANANA TEA BREAD

2⅔ cups sifted all-purpose flour

3½ teaspoons double-acting baking powder

¾ teaspoon salt

½ cup butter or margarine

¼ teaspoon baking soda

½ teaspoon grated lemon rind

1 cup sugar

3 eggs

¾ cup white raisins

1½ cups mashed ripe bananas

Sift flour with baking powder and salt. Set aside.

Combine butter, soda, and grated lemon rind. Gradually blend in sugar, mixing until light and fluffy. Beat in eggs, one at a time. Stir in raisins. Add flour mixture alternately with bananas.

Turn into a well-greased, lightly floured 9x5x3-inch loaf pan. Bake in a 350° F. oven 1 hour and 10 minutes or until done.

Makes 1 loaf.

ALMOND BREAD

2 cups sifted all-purpose flour
1 tablespoon baking powder
¼ teaspoon ground cinnamon
1 cup brown sugar
2 eggs, slightly beaten

2 tablespoons melted butter or margarine
¼ teaspoon pure vanilla extract
1 square unsweetened chocolate, grated
1 cup chopped blanched almonds

Sift together flour, baking powder, and cinnamon.

Add sugar gradually to beaten eggs, mixing well. Add butter or margarine and vanilla extract. Stir in grated chocolate and almonds.

Add flour mixture to egg mixture. Blend well.

Pat into 2 greased 9-inch round cake pans. Bake in a 375° F. oven about 20 minutes.

While still warm, cut into strips or wedge-shaped pieces.

Makes two 9-inch breads.

BANANA NUT BREAD

1¼ cups granulated brown sugar
½ teaspoon salt
⅓ cup soft butter or margarine
2 eggs
2¼ cups sifted all-purpose flour

1 teaspoon double-acting baking powder
1½ teaspoons baking soda
¼ teaspoon nutmeg
1 cup ripe mashed bananas
½ cup buttermilk
1 cup chopped pecans or walnuts

Cream sugar, salt, and butter thoroughly in large mixing bowl. Beat eggs into mixture, one at a time until light and fluffy.

Sift together flour, baking powder, soda, and nutmeg. Combine bananas and milk. Add parts of dry and liquid ingredients alternately to creamed ingredients, blending well after each addition. Add nuts; mix briefly.

Turn into greased 9x5-inch loaf pan. Bake in a 350° F. oven about 80 minutes or until cake tester comes out clean. Remove to cooling rack. When cool, wrap in foil or clear plastic wrap.

Makes 1 loaf.

FRESH TANGERINE NUT LOAF

2 cups sifted all-purpose flour
¾ teaspoon baking soda
1 teaspoon baking powder
½ teaspoon salt
1 teaspoon nutmeg or mace
¼ cup grated tangerine peel
¾ cup fresh tangerine juice
⅓ cup butter or margarine, melted
1 egg, beaten
1 cup sugar
¼ cup chopped raisins
½ cup coarsely chopped nuts

Sift flour, soda, baking powder, salt, and nutmeg or mace.

In bowl, combine grated tangerine peel, tangerine juice, melted butter or margarine, beaten egg, sugar, and raisins, blending well. Stir in flour mixture, beating until just mixed; add nuts.

Spoon into greased 9x5x3-inch loaf pan. Bake in a 350° F. oven 50 to 60 minutes. Remove from pan; cool on rack.

Makes 1 loaf.

STICKY CINNAMON ROLLS

ROLLS:

½ cup granulated sugar
1 package active dry
   yeast
¼ cup lukewarm water
1 egg
1 cup lukewarm milk
⅓ cup shortening,
   softened
½ teaspoon salt

3¾ cups sifted all-
   purpose flour
Melted shortening or
   salad oil
Sugar and cinnamon
⅔ cup seedless raisins
¾ cup chopped pecans or
   walnuts

GLAZE:

1½ cups granulated brown
   sugar
2 tablespoons water
¼ cup butter or
   margarine

3 tablespoons light corn
   syrup
¼ teaspoon salt
Pecan or walnut halves

Roll dough: Mix granulated sugar and yeast in large mixing bowl. Add lukewarm water; stir mixture until dissolved. Blend egg, warm milk, shortening, and salt into yeast mixture. Add flour, about ⅓ at a time, blending well. Cover; allow to rise in warm place about 1 hour.

Glaze: Combine brown sugar, water, butter or margarine, corn syrup, and salt in 1-quart saucepan. Bring to boil, stirring constantly. Remove from heat. Place 2 teaspoons glaze and nut halves in well-greased muffin-pan cups. Set muffin pans aside for later use.

Rolls: When dough has doubled bulk, turn onto floured board and knead. Divide dough in half. Roll half of dough into 8x15-inch rectangle. Brush with melted shortening.

Sprinkle with sugar and cinnamon and half of raisins and nuts. Form dough into long roll; secure edge by moistening and pressing to roll. Repeat with second half of dough.

Cut in 1¼-inch slices; arrange in muffin cups. Cover loosely, allow to rise 1 hour in warm place or until light. Brush lightly with melted shortening. Bake in 425° F. oven 13 minutes or until done. Turn rolls onto cooling rack over tray or waxed paper. When cool, store rolls in semi-airtight container with waxed paper between layers.

Makes 24 rolls.

ORANGE CINNAMON YEAST ROLLS

1 *cup sugar*
2 *teaspoons ground cinnamon*
2 *tablespoons grated orange peel*
3 *tablespoons fresh orange juice*

¼ *cup butter or margarine*
1 *package active dry yeast*
¾ *cup warm water*
2½ *cups packaged biscuit mix*

In saucepan combine sugar, cinnamon, orange peel, orange juice, and butter or margarine; bring to boil, stirring constantly, and cook for 2 minutes. Cool.

Dissolve yeast in warm water; stir in biscuit mix, beating vigorously. Turn dough onto pastry cloth or breadboard dusted with additional biscuit mix or flour; knead about 20 times or until smooth.

Roll dough into rectangle, 8x16 inches. Spread ⅓ to ½ cup of the cooled syrup on the rolled dough, spreading within ½ inch of the edge. Roll up tightly jelly-roll fashion beginning at long side. Seal well by pinching edges of roll together. Cut roll into 1-inch crosswise slices. Spoon remaining syrup into greased muffin-pan cups. Place cut rolls in muffin cups. Cover and let rise until double in bulk.

Bake in a 350° F. oven 25 to 30 minutes.

Makes 1 dozen rolls.

BUTTERSCOTCH CRUMB BISCUITS

1 can refrigerator biscuits
½ cup granulated brown sugar
½ teaspoon water

1 tablespoon butter or margarine
2 tablespoons finely chopped nuts

Arrange biscuits in greased 8-inch round baking pan.

Blend sugar, water, and butter; add nuts. Sprinkle mixture over biscuits.

Bake in a 475° F. oven 10 minutes or until golden brown.

Makes 10 biscuits.

CINNAMON BANANA MUFFINS

2 cups sifted all-purpose flour
1 teaspoon salt
2 teaspoons double-acting baking powder
1½ teaspoons ground cinnamon
⅓ cup sugar
1 egg, well beaten

1 cup milk
¼ cup vegetable shortening, melted
1 cup mashed ripe bananas
¼ teaspoon ground cinnamon
1 tablespoon sugar

Sift flour, salt, baking powder, cinnamon, and sugar into mixing bowl.

Combine egg, milk, and shortening. Add to dry ingredients. Add mashed bananas and stir until all ingredients are blended. Batter will be lumpy.

Fill greased muffin-pan cups ¾ full.

Combine remaining cinnamon and sugar. Sprinkle over top of each muffin.

Bake in a 425° F. oven 20 to 25 minutes.

Makes 12 2½-inch muffins.

CINNAMON TEA BISCUITS

2 cups sifted all-purpose flour

3 teaspoons double-acting baking powder

1 teaspoon salt

¼ cup vegetable shortening

½ cup milk

⅓ cup butter or margarine

1½ teaspoons ground cinnamon

½ cup sugar

Melted butter or margarine

Sift flour with baking powder and salt. Cut in shortening. Add milk and stir until a soft dough forms. Turn out onto a lightly floured board.

Knead lightly about 20 seconds. Roll dough into a rectangle ⅛ inch thick.

Mix butter or margarine with cinnamon and sugar. Spread mixture over dough. Roll up jelly-roll fashion and cut into 1-inch slices. Place in greased muffin-pan cups. Brush tops with melted butter or margarine.

Bake in a 400° F. oven 15 to 20 minutes.

Makes 16 biscuits.

PEANUT BUTTER MUFFINS

1¾ cups sifted all-
purpose flour
¼ cup sugar
1 tablespoon baking
powder
½ teaspoon salt

1 cup milk
¼ cup peanut butter
1 egg
1 tablespoon butter or
margarine, melted

Sift dry ingredients together.

Combine milk, peanut butter, egg, and margarine. Pour at once into dry ingredients. Stir with fork until ingredients are just blended.

Spoon into 12 greased muffin-pan cups. Bake in a 400° F. oven 20 minutes.

Makes 12 muffins.

FRENCH BREAD

2 cups warm (not hot)
water
1 package active dry
yeast or
1 cake compressed yeast

1 tablespoon sugar
2 teaspoons salt
5¾ cups sifted all-
purpose flour
1 egg white, unbeaten

Measure warm (not hot) water into warmed bowl. Sprinkle dry yeast over water. (Crumble compressed yeast into lukewarm water.) Stir until dissolved. Add sugar, salt, and 3 cups flour. Stir to mix, then beat until smooth and shiny. Stir in 2½ cups more flour.

Sprinkle remaining ¼ cup flour on pastry cloth or breadboard. Turn dough out on flour and knead until satiny smooth, 5 to 7 minutes. Shape into smooth ball.

Rub bowl lightly with shortening. Press top of ball of dough into greased bowl, then turn dough over. Cover with waxed paper, then clean towel. Let rise until doubled (about 1 hour).

Punch down. Divide into halves. Shape each half into a ball. Cover and let rest 5 minutes.

Rub a little shortening on palms of hands. Then roll each ball of dough under the hands to form a long slender loaf about 3 inches in diameter. Start rolling at the center and gently work hands toward ends of loaf. Do this several times to make well-shaped loaves.

Place loaves 4 inches apart on lightly greased baking sheet. With sharp knife cut diagonal gashes about ¾ inch deep about 1½ inches apart into top of each loaf. Cover and let rise until a little more than doubled (about 1 hour).

Bake in 425° F. oven 30 to 35 minutes. Remove from oven. Brush with egg white. Return to oven for 2 minutes.

Remove from baking sheet and cool on rack or across tops of pans.

Makes 2 loaves.

SWEDISH LIMPE

1½ cups water, divided	½ cup warm (not hot) water
¼ cup brown sugar, firmly packed	1 package active dry yeast
2 teaspoons caraway seeds	or
2 tablespoons vegetable shortening	1 cake compressed yeast
2 teaspoons salt	4 cups sifted white flour
	2 cups sifted rye flour

Into small saucepan, measure ½ cup water, brown sugar, caraway seeds, shortening, and salt. Bring to boil and simmer gently 5 minutes. Remove from heat and pour into large mixing bowl. Add 1 cup cold water.

Into cup or small bowl measure ½ cup warm (not hot) water. Sprinkle dry yeast over water. (Crumble compressed yeast into lukewarm water.) Stir until dissolved. After yeast dissolves, stir 2 cups white flour into liquid in large bowl. Add dissolved yeast and mix well. Stir in remaining 2 cups white flour. Mix well. Stir in 1½ cups rye flour, reserving remaining ½ cup rye flour for kneading.

Sprinkle ¼ cup rye flour on pastry cloth or breadboard. Turn dough out on floured cloth or board and knead until smooth and satiny. Use the remaining ¼ cup rye flour if dough feels sticky and too soft. Place ball of dough into greased bowl, first pressing top of dough into bowl to coat it lightly with fat. Turn ball over. Cover and let rise until doubled (about 1¼ hours). Punch down. (For a finer grained bread, let dough rise a second time until doubled.) Divide dough into halves. Shape each half into a ball. Place on lightly greased baking sheet about 4 inches apart. If desired, make 3 or 4 cuts ½ inch deep with sharp knife across tops of loaves. Cover and let rise until doubled (about 1 hour).

Bake in 400° F. oven 45 to 50 minutes. Remove from baking sheet and cool on racks or across tops of bread pans away from drafts.

For a shiny crust, brush tops of loaves with milk or egg white when done, and return to oven for 2 minutes. If preferred, dough may be shaped in regular loaves and baked in bread pans.

Makes 2 loaves.

GUGELHUPF

½ cup milk
1 package active dry
    yeast or
1 cake compressed yeast
¼ cup warm (not hot)
    water
½ cup sugar
½ teaspoon salt
2 eggs
½ cup melted butter or
    margarine
2½ cups sifted all-purpose
    flour

½ cup chopped raisins
1 teaspoon grated lemon
    rind
For Pan:
1 tablespoon margarine or
    butter
2 tablespoons fine bread
    crumbs or finely ground
    almonds
16 whole blanched
    almonds

Scald milk. Pour into mixing bowl and cool until it is warm (not hot). While milk cools, sprinkle dry yeast into warm water in cup. (Crumble compressed yeast into lukewarm water.) Stir until dissolved. To milk in bowl add sugar, salt, and 1½ cups flour. Mix well. Add dissolved yeast and beat until smooth. Add eggs and beat thoroughly. If you prefer, beat the eggs first in a separate bowl. Add melted and cooled butter or margarine, about a tablespoon at a time, mixing it in well before adding more. Stir in remaining 1¼ cups flour.

Then beat batter about 5 minutes. (An electric mixer set at moderate speed is good for this.) With rubber scraper scrape batter down from side of bowl. Cover and let rise in warm place until doubled (about 1½ hours).

While batter rises prepare baking pan. Use either a fancy mold that holds a quart or 2 1-pint molds, or a 7-inch angel food cake pan. Rub the inside of the pan generously with butter or margarine. Then sprinkle fine white bread crumbs into the pan. Shake it to coat the whole inside of the pan with crumbs. Arrange almonds in a design in bottom of pan.

When batter has doubled, stir it down. Mix in the raisins and lemon rind. Carefully spoon the batter on top of the almonds so as not to spoil your design. When all the batter is in the pan, cover and let rise in warm place until doubled (about 1¼ hours).

Bake in 350° F. oven 45 to 50 minutes. Look at the cake after it has baked 15 minutes. If it is turning brown, place a piece of clean brown wrapping paper over the top for the rest of the baking period. This is a rich batter and browns easily.

When done, turn out of pan on wire cake rack. If you wish, dust lightly with confectioners' sugar. To make a design on top of the cake, place a scalloped lace paper doily on the cake and sift confectioners' sugar over it. Lift the doily carefully and pour the extra sugar back into the container.

Makes 1 cake.

SALLY LUNN

¾ cup milk
2 tablespoons sugar
1 teaspoon salt
2 tablespoons vegetable shortening
1 package active dry yeast
   or

1 cake compressed yeast
¼ cup warm (not hot) water
2¾ cups sifted all-purpose flour
1 egg

Scald milk. Add sugar, salt, and shortening. Stir to dissolve. Pour into mixing bowl. Cool to lukewarm.

While milk cools, sprinkle dry yeast into warm (not hot) water. Stir until dissolved. (Crumble compressed yeast into lukewarm water.) To cooled milk add 2 cups flour. Mix well, then beat until smooth.

Stir in dissolved yeast. Add egg and beat at least 1 minute. Stir in remaining flour and beat until smooth (about 2 minutes). Scrape batter down from side of bowl. Cover and let rise until doubled (about 1 hour). Stir down and turn batter into greased 9-inch round cake pan 1½ inches deep, or into 4½x2¾x9-inch loaf pan. Let rise until doubled (about 1 hour).

Bake in a 350° F. oven 45 minutes. Turn out on rack. Cool slightly. Serve warm, with margarine or butter and marmalade. Separate pieces with two forks.

Makes 1 loaf.

TEA PARTY CANDIES

BRANDIED PEANUTS

1½ cups peanuts
½ cup sifted confec-
  tioners' sugar
1 tablespoon peanut oil

1 tablespoon milk
1½ teaspoons brandy
  flavoring

Heat peanuts thoroughly in a 350° F. oven.

In a bowl, mix together until smooth confectioners' sugar, oil, milk, and brandy flavoring. Stir hot peanuts into sugar mixture until nuts are well coated. Spread out on waxed paper to cool.

Makes 1½ cups.

PERSIAN BONBONS

4 egg whites
½ teaspoon salt
1¼ cups sugar

1 teaspoon almond
  extract
2 cups flaked coconut
Crystallized ginger

Combine egg whites and salt; beat until frothy. Add sugar, a tablespoon at a time, beating until stiff and glossy. Add almond extract and coconut, mixing lightly.

Drop by teaspoonfuls onto greased and floured baking sheet. Bake in a 350° F. oven 20 minutes. Loosen with spatula; remove to wire racks.

Top each immediately with a small piece of ginger.

Makes about 5 dozen bonbons.

PEANUT RUM BALLS

2½ cups finely crushed
vanilla wafers (about
5½ dozen)
1 cup sifted confectioners'
sugar

½ cup chopped peanuts
2 tablespoons cocoa
3 tablespoons corn syrup
¼ cup rum
Confectioners' sugar

Combine crushed vanilla wafers, sifted confectioners' sugar, chopped peanuts, and cocoa; mix well. Add corn syrup and rum. Mix until blended.

Shape into 1-inch balls, then roll in confectioners' sugar.

Makes about 3 dozen rum balls.

NO-COOK FONDANT

⅓ cup soft butter or
margarine
⅓ cup light corn syrup
½ teaspoon salt

1 teaspoon pure vanilla
extract
4½ cups sifted
confectioners' sugar

Blend margarine, corn syrup, salt, and vanilla extract in large mixing bowl. Add sifted confectioners' sugar all at once. Mix

166

all together, first with spoon, and then with hands knead in dry ingredients.

Turn onto board and continue kneading until mixture is well blended and smooth. Store in a cool place.

Makes about 1⅓ pounds candy.

VARIATIONS

Mint Patties: Substitute 1 teaspoon peppermint or wintergreen flavoring for vanilla extract. Tint to desired color, using red vegetable coloring for wintergreen and green coloring for peppermint. Shape into balls; or roll thin and cut into any shape desired.

Orange or Lemon Creams: Substitute 2 teaspoons orange extract or 1 teaspoon lemon extract for vanilla extract. Tint to a delicious orange or yellow using vegetable coloring. Shape as above.

Almond Diamonds: Substitute 1 teaspoon almond extract for vanilla extract. Add ½ cup coarsely chopped blanched and toasted almonds. Roll out or pat to ½-inch thickness. Cut into diamonds.

Candied Fruit Squares: If desired, rum or rum extract may be substituted for vanilla extract. Add ½ cup finely chopped mixed candied fruit. Roll; cut into squares.

Mocha Logs: Add 2 teaspoons powdered instant coffee. Shape into small rolls about ½ inch in diameter and 2 inches long. Roll in chocolate candy cake decorations.

TEN-MINUTE FUDGE

3 squares (1 ounce each) unsweetened chocolate

4 tablespoons butter or margarine

4½ cups sifted confectioners' sugar

⅓ cup instant nonfat dry milk

½ cup light or dark corn syrup

1 tablespoon water

1 teaspoon pure vanilla extract

½ cup chopped nuts (optional)

Melt chocolate and margarine in top of 2-quart double boiler over hot water. Meanwhile sift together confectioners' sugar and dry milk.

Stir corn syrup, water, and vanilla extract into chocolate-margarine mixture. Stir in sifted sugar and dry milk in 2 additions. Continue stirring until mixture is well blended and smooth.

Remove from heat. Stir in nuts. Turn into greased square 8x8x2-inch pan. Cool. Cut into squares.

Makes 1¾ pounds candy.

Brown Sugar Fudge: Follow recipe for Ten-Minute Fudge omitting chocolate and water. Melt ½ cup brown sugar with the margarine. Use dark corn syrup.

OLD-FASHIONED CHOCOLATE FUDGE

3 tablespoons butter or
  margarine
3 cups sugar
2 tablespoons light or
  dark corn syrup
2 squares unsweetened
  chocolate

¾ cup milk
1 teaspoon pure vanilla
  extract
1 cup walnuts, coarsely
  chopped (optional)

Place margarine, sugar, corn syrup, chocolate, and milk in heavy 3-quart saucepan. Cook over medium heat, stirring constantly, until mixture boils. Continue cooking, stirring occasionally, to soft-ball stage (238° F.) or until a small amount of mixture forms a soft ball when tested in cold water.

Remove from heat. Add vanilla extract. Cool to lukewarm (110° F.). Beat until fudge begins to thicken and loses its gloss. Fold in nuts.

Quickly pour into greased 8x8x2-inch pan. For best results do not spread fudge or scrape out of pan. When cold, cut in squares.

Makes 2 pounds candy.

QUICK PEANUT BUTTER FUDGE

⅓ cup butter or
  margarine
½ cup dark corn syrup
¾ cup peanut butter
½ teaspoon salt

1 teaspoon pure vanilla
  extract
4½ cups sifted
  confectioners' sugar
¾ cup chopped nuts

Blend butter, corn syrup, peanut butter, salt, and vanilla in large mixing bowl. Stir in sifted confectioners' sugar gradually.

Turn onto board and knead until well blended and smooth. Add nuts gradually, pressing and kneading into candy.

Press out with hands or rolling pin into a square ½ inch thick. Cut into serving pieces.

Makes about 2 pounds candy.

QUICK POPCORN BALLS

¼ cup corn oil
½ cup popcorn
½ cup dark corn syrup

½ cup sugar
½ teaspoon salt

Heat corn oil in a 4-quart kettle over medium heat for 3 minutes. Add popcorn. Cover, leaving small air space at edge of cover. Shake frequently over medium heat until popping stops.

Meanwhile, mix together dark corn syrup, sugar, and salt. Add to popped corn in kettle and stir constantly over medium heat 3 to 5 minutes or until corn is evenly and completely coated with mixture. Remove from heat.

Form into balls, using as little pressure as possible. Use margarine on hands, if desired.

Makes 6 popcorn balls about 2½ inches in diameter.

Note: Do not double recipe.

Caramel Corns: Follow above recipe. After removing from heat, spread on waxed paper and separate the pieces of popped corn. Makes about 2 quarts.

Pastel Popcorn Balls: Follow recipe for Quick Popcorn Balls, using light corn syrup for dark corn syrup, and tint corn-syrup mixture with pink or green vegetable coloring before adding popped corn. Flavor green syrup with peppermint, and the pink syrup with wintergreen.

DIVINITY

½ cup light corn syrup
2½ cups sugar
¼ teaspoon salt
½ cup water

2 egg whites
1 teaspoon pure vanilla extract
1 cup coarsely chopped nuts (optional)

Combine corn syrup, sugar, salt, and water in saucepan. Cook over medium heat, stirring constantly, until sugar is dissolved. Cook, without stirring, to firm-ball stage (248° F.) or until a small amount of syrup forms a firm ball which does not flatten when dropped into very cold water.

Just before syrup reaches 248° F., beat egg whites with electric mixer or rotary beater until stiff but not dry. Pour about one half of the syrup slowly over egg whites, beating constantly. Cook the remainder of the syrup to soft-crack stage (272° F.) or until a small amount of syrup separates into threads which are hard but not brittle when dropped into very cold water.

Add syrup slowly to the first mixture, beating constantly. Continue beating until mixture holds its shape. If mixture becomes too heavy for beater, continue beating with a wooden spoon. Add vanilla extract and nuts.

Drop from tip of spoon onto waxed paper.

Makes about 1¼ pounds candy.

MINTED WALNUTS

¼ cup light corn syrup
1 cup sugar
½ cup water
1 teaspoon essence of
   peppermint

10 marshmallows
3 cups (10 ounces)
   walnut halves

Combine corn syrup, sugar, and water in a saucepan. Cook over medium heat, stirring constantly until mixture boils. Continue cooking to soft-ball stage (238° F.) or until a small amount of mixture forms a soft ball when tested in very cold water. Remove from heat; quickly add essence of peppermint and marshmallows. Stir until marshmallows are dissolved.

Add walnut halves. Stir until walnuts are well coated.

Pour onto waxed paper. Separate walnut halves while still warm.

Makes 1¼ pounds candy.

VANILLA TAFFY

1 cup sugar
¾ cup dark corn syrup
½ cup water
¼ teaspoon cream of
   tartar

1 teaspoon pure vanilla
   extract
1 tablespoon butter or
   margarine

Combine sugar, corn syrup, water, and cream of tartar in saucepan. Bring to a boil over medium heat, stirring constantly until sugar dissolves. Continue cooking without stirring, to hard-ball stage (266° F.) or until a small amount of mixture forms a hard ball when tested in very cold water.

Remove from heat; stir in vanilla extract and butter.

Pour into greased 8x8x2-inch square pan; let stand until cool enough to handle.

Pull candy with fingers until it has a satinlike finish and milky-white color. Pull into long strips ¾ inch in diameter. Cut into 1-inch pieces with scissors. Wrap in waxed paper.

Makes about ½ pound candy.

CANDIED ORANGE PEEL

2 medium oranges   1 cup granulated sugar
1 teaspoon salt   1 cup water
½ cup dark corn syrup

Select thick-skinned oranges of a good color and free from blemishes. Wash oranges, remove peel in 4 to 6 sections. Cover peel with cold water; add salt. Bring to a boil; boil 10 minutes. Drain. Repeat operations 3 times, omitting salt.

With bowl of spoon, after each cooking period, gently scrape off moist white membrane. Peel should be about ¼ inch thick. Cut peel into strips.

Combine corn syrup, sugar, and water in 3-quart saucepan. Cook over medium heat, stirring constantly, until sugar is dissolved. Add orange peel; bring to a boil. Reduce heat and boil gently 45 minutes.

Drain in coarse strainer or colander, reserving syrup. Bring syrup to a full rolling boil. Cool; store covered in refrigerator.

Roll peel, a few pieces at a time, in sugar. Arrange in a single layer on trays; let dry about 24 hours. Store covered.

Makes about 1 pound peel.

Note: Use syrup as a dessert sauce or for pancakes.

Chocolate-Tipped: Melt ½ cup chocolate semisweet bits in top of double boiler over hot water. Dip ends of peel. Put on waxed paper until chocolate is hardened.

SPICED GLACÉ NUTS

1½ cups sugar
1 teaspoon ground cinnamon
¼ teaspoon ground cloves
⅛ teaspoon ground ginger
⅛ teaspoon ground nutmeg

½ cup light or dark corn syrup
½ cup water
½ teaspoon salt
3 cups nuts
2 tablespoons butter or margarine

Combine sugar, spices, corn syrup, water, and salt in heavy saucepan. Stir over low heat until sugar is dissolved, then cook over medium heat, without stirring, to hard-crack stage (300° F.) or until a small amount of syrup separates into threads which are hard and brittle when dropped into very cold water.

Meanwhile, spread nuts into shallow pan and heat in 350° F. oven for 10 minutes. Reduce heat under candy mixture to very low. Add heated nuts and margarine. Stir just until nuts are coated and margarine is melted.

Remove from heat. Turn out into large coarse sieve, set over a pan for 1 minute to drain off excess syrup, then spread nuts on greased pan and separate with forks. If desired, saucepan can be placed over boiling water to keep warm and nuts removed separately with forks onto greased pan.

PEANUT BRITTLE

1 cup light or dark corn syrup
1/8 teaspoon salt
1 cup sugar
1/4 cup water
2 tablespoons butter or margarine
1 1/2 cups shelled peanuts
2 teaspoons hot water
1 teaspoon baking soda

Stir together corn syrup, salt, sugar, water, and butter. Cook to soft-crack stage (280° F.) or until a small amount separates into threads which are hard but not brittle when tested in very cold water.

Stir in peanuts gradually so that mixture will continue to boil. Cook, stirring frequently, to hard-crack stage (300° F.) or until a small amount separates into threads which are hard and brittle when tested in very cold water. Color of mixture will darken slightly.

Remove from heat. Stir hot water into baking soda and beat thoroughly into brittle.

Turn out onto heavily greased baking sheet and with spatula spread as thin as possible. Let cool slightly, about 5 minutes, then turn warm brittle upside down. Sheet of brittle may be cut into strips to make it easier to turn. Stretch brittle to desired thickness. With this method the nuts are covered more evenly with brittle mixture. Let cool, break into irregular shaped pieces.

Makes about 1 1/4 pounds candy.

CARAMELS

1 cup sugar
1 cup light or dark corn syrup
1 cup light cream
1/4 cup butter or margarine

Measure sugar, syrup, cream, and butter in heavy 3-quart saucepan. Cook over medium heat, stirring constantly, until sugar is dissolved and mixture boils. Continue cooking, stirring occasionally, until mixture thickens, then cook over low heat stirring constantly to prevent scorching, to firm-ball stage (244° F.) or until a small amount of mixture when dropped into very cold water forms a firm ball which does not flatten on removal from water.

Pour into lightly buttered 8x8x2-inch pan. When set but still warm, mark off caramels of desired size and shape.

When cool, turn block of candy onto cutting board and cut where marked. (If candy sticks to pan, heat bottom of pan slightly to loosen; remove from pan and cool candy before cutting). Wrap in waxed paper.

Makes about 1 pound candy.

MARSHMALLOWS

1 envelope unflavored
   gelatine
⅓ cup cold water
½ cup granulated sugar
⅔ cup light corn syrup

½ teaspoon pure vanilla
   extract
Cornstarch
Powdered sugar

Soften gelatine in cold water in a small saucepan. Place saucepan over boiling water and stir until gelatine is dissolved. Add sugar and stir until sugar is dissolved.

Pour syrup into large bowl (3- to 4-quart) of electric mixer. Add vanilla extract, gelatine-and-sugar mixture, and beat about 15 minutes or until mixture becomes thick and of a marshmallow consistency.

Cover thoroughly bottom of 7x10x1½-inch pan with equal parts cornstarch and fine powdered sugar. Pour marshmallow mixture into pan and smooth off top with a knife. Let stand in a cool place (not refrigerator) until well set, about 1 hour.

To remove from pan, loosen around edges with a knife, invert over a board sprinkled lightly with equal parts of cornstarch and fine powdered sugar. Cut into squares with a sharp knife, moistened with cold water. Roll in equal parts cornstarch and fine powdered sugar.

Makes about 1 pound candy.

CANDIED TANGERINE PEEL

6 medium to large tangerines	3 tablespoons light corn syrup
Cold water	1 cup water
¼ teaspoon salt	½ cup confectioners' sugar
1½ cups sugar	

Wash tangerines; cut unpeeled fruit into quarters. Separate fruit from peel, leaving peel intact. Save tangerine meat for salads or snacks. Cut peel into thin slivers, 1 to 1½ inches long. Cover peel with cold water in large saucepan. Bring to boil, uncovered, and cook at medium boil 15 to 20 minutes, or until peel is tender. Drain.

In saucepan, combine salt, sugar, corn syrup, and water; bring to boil. Add drained tangerine peel. Simmer uncovered until syrup is almost absorbed by peel, 25 to 30 minutes. Remove from heat. Allow peel to set in pan until almost cool. Drain peel and place on rack to dry overnight.

Roll peel in confectioners' sugar. Store in covered container in refrigerator.

Makes approximately ½ pound candied peel.

INDEX

H37

10/93 15
7/99. 36
4/13 −53